Simon Peter

Eleanor Snyder

FAITH & LIFE PRESS

Newton, Kansas
Winnipeg, Manitoba

Published by the General Conference Mennonite
Church, Commission on Education, Newton, Kansas.
Elizabeth Raid Pankratz, editor; Mary Gaeddert, copy
editor; John Hiebert, cover and design; David Ediger,
illustrator.

Printed in the U.S.A.

Library of Congress Catalogue Number 94-61288

ISBN 0-87303-234-9

Table of Contents

Look It Over

Look it over

Meet the writer

Eleanor Snyder serves as Director of Children's Education for the Commission on Education of the General Conference Mennonite Church, Newton, Kansas.

Eleanor enjoys designing children's curriculum for use in congregations. She has been involved in writing vacation Bible school materials in her local congregation and the Mennonite Conference of Eastern Canada for many years. She is an active member of Bloomingdale Mennonite Church, Bloomingdale, Ontario. She is married to Stuart and has two young adult children, Jeff and Sheila.

Writing *Simon Peter* was a collaborative effort of dedicated and energetic Christian educators. This team met regularly to brainstorm and develop the curriculum. Sincere thanks and appreciation goes to the following people for their creative and voluntary contributions: Phyllis Bishop, games; Elizabeth Eby, the early childhood puppet plays; Clare Jantzi, craft ideas; Elaine Leis, music resources; Elsie Martin, story application and memory suggestions; Susan Pries, early childhood sessions and music; Louise Shoemaker, ideas for early childhood sessions; and Jock Tolmay, dramas and illustrations.

Simon Peter is the fourth piece in the Living Stones Collection of complete, freestanding children's curriculum. Both *Simon Peter* and *I Am Somebody God Loves* from this collection are designed for use by children age 3 through grade 8.

Through Bible stories about Peter's journey with Jesus from fisherman to follower to leader in the early church, the children will experience Jesus' love for them and his presence in their lives. Hands-on activities reinforce the Bible stories and help the children apply Peter's experiences with Jesus to their lives.

Materials include Bible story dramas, puppet plays, activity sheets, patterns, memory work, organizational forms, and student take-home pieces that can be photocopied. Complete lesson plans, games, songs, and helpful illustrations make this curriculum easy and fun to teach.

I hope that together with the children you will experience God's love and care as you teach and learn from *Simon Peter*. May your personal relationship with God be strengthened, and may you experience Jesus' presence as you teach this curriculum. May you find joy in serving and learning together with the children.

Elizabeth Raid Pankratz, editor

The writer encourages

Simon Peter provides an experience-based biblical curriculum for congregations wishing to explore new ways of teaching and learning with children. *Simon Peter* follows the integrated learning approach of *I Am Somebody God Loves* and presents the material in a user-friendly format. The new function-based Resource sections are already organized for each session and ready to use.

We chose to tell Peter's story for several reasons. Peter's life changed dramatically as a result of a growing relationship with Jesus. His story begins with an invitation to change from a fisherman to a follower of Jesus and ends with his willingness to accept all people into God's family. Each story illustrates a transforming moment in Peter's life as a result of his friendship with Jesus. Jesus invited and challenged Peter to be a faithful follower throughout his whole life.

The Bible story is central to each session. The activities are integrated to support the Bible story and session theme. In Then and Now children apply the truths of the story through discussion, role-plays, dramas, memory verses, and creative expression. Make and Take provides hands-on activities that reinforce the story for children who learn best by doing and making. Games and Snacks involves active learning through games and cooperative activities. While they eat a snack together, children are encouraged to make connections between the games and Peter's story.

Enjoy this curriculum with the children. If you, as a leader, are having a good time learning about Peter and Jesus, the children will capture your enthusiam. Build relationships. Model Christian discipleship. Learn about the friendship of Jesus offered to each one of us. Jesus invites you and me to be his friend and follower.

May God's Holy Spirit transform and guide you as you learn together about Peter's transforming friendship with Jesus, the Christ.

Eleanor Snyder, writer

Theme

Simon Peter: From Fisherman to Follower to Leader

In this curriculum, children and leaders will learn about Simon Peter and his transformation from a fisherman to a courageous leader in the early church as a follower of Jesus Christ. Peter's story begins with the invitation to follow Jesus as a disciple and ends with his willingness to accept all people into God's family. Each day we will look at a different transformation, or one might say *conversion*, in the life of a simple follower of Jesus. The session themes include the following:

Session 1: *From Fisherman to Follower*
Session 2: *From Faith to Failure to Faith*
Session 3: *From Loyalty to Betrayal*
Session 4: *From Fear to Courage*
Session 5: *From Rejection to Acceptance*

Included for each day are appropriate biblical texts that provide background reading for the leaders, a specific theme, story and faith focus, song titles, Bible stories in drama form, plans for three rotating activity sessions, as well as alternative activities.

There is a separate section for each of three age groupings: early childhood (ages 3, 4, and 5), kindergarten (completed) to grade 5, and junior youth (grades 6, 7, and 8). All groups will use the same texts and themes each day.

The Bible memory passage is 2 Peter 1:3, 5-7. Ideas and activities for memorizing this passage are found throughout the session plans.

Objectives

1. To familiarize children with the biblical character of Simon Peter. Peter showed that one does not have to be perfect to become a follower of Jesus. God can, through a relationship with the Holy Spirit, help each of us to become more Christ-like.

2. To encourage children to accept Jesus' invitation to be his personal friend in age-appropriate ways.

3. To help children understand that God will make a difference in our lives if we are open to the prompting of the Holy Spirit.

4. To provide an alternative to the "schooling" method of teaching by providing group interaction and experiential learning activities for children from early childhood through junior youth.

5. To integrate all activities under a common theme. Arts and crafts, games, songs, and responses to the story are connected to the daily topic and reinforce the theme in a variety of ways. In Deuteronomy 6, adults are encouraged to teach their children about God all the time. The "teachable moment" may come during crafts and games as well as during the Bible story or discussion.

Methods

This programme is designed for five sessions, each lasting 2 3/4 hours. The setting is adaptable—out-of-doors, inside, or a combination of both. If your programme does not allow for this length of time, consider these options: shorten Gather and Greet and Gather and Bless, shorten the time for worship, or offer two rotation activities. For a detailed outline, refer to the Master Schedule on page 22.

Adapt it

This curriculum is designed for fourteen hours of solid Christian education. Decide how these materials can be used best in your setting.

Consider uses other than vacation Bible school. The versatility of this curriculum allows for use in Sunday school, midweek programmes, camping programmes, and all-church worship and education events.

Summer Sunday school

Try it for a summer Sunday school programme. Many churches are using broadly graded groupings of children rather than single-grade groups during the summer. This plan provides variety for the children and can accommodate the fluctuating numbers of children attending. Fewer leaders are required, thus giving regular teachers a change of pace or a break from teaching.

Choose from these ideas of how to use this curriculum with children from early childhood through grade 8. If your church has enough young children, it is recommended that you group them separately and use the Early Childhood section, pages 113-159.

For a five-week course:

Use one session each Sunday. Present the Bible story dramatically to the larger group of children (kindergarten through junior youth). Then break into smaller age groups for discussion and story reinforcement using the daily suggestions in Then and Now, pages 61-80. End each session with a variety of centres for children to respond in a personal way to the story. Use the ideas in Make and Take, pages 97-112, or additional suggestions from Then and Now.

For a ten-week course:

Use one session for two Sundays. Present the Bible story on both Sundays. If that is not possible, videotape the first Sunday's presentation and show the video the second Sunday. This offers a review of the story for those who have already seen it and gets newcomers on board with the theme of the day. Offer a variety of response activity centres and let the children choose. Centres can be the same both weeks, or additional centres may be set up. To provide closure, use the games from Games and Snacks, pages 81-96, on the second Sunday.

For a thirteen-week course:

Follow the plan for a ten-week course. For the three additional sessions, plan celebration Sundays. On the first Sunday, introduce the theme, learn the theme songs, and whet the children's enthusiasm by presenting some clips from the dramas and/or playing a game or two.

Use the last two Sundays in the summer to celebrate and wrap up. One Sunday, invite children to share their learning. Using skits, art, poetry, etc., have the children tell each other what they learned from Peter and his relationship with Jesus. Children can show what they made. A videotape of the various activities over the summer sessions could be shown.

On the last Sunday, celebrate the friendship of Jesus through games and stories. Play favourite games from the curriculum. Review the theme by telling or reading the stories not used earlier. Invite some adults to tell how their friendship with Jesus has changed their lives. End by sharing a snack and singing songs. Close with a prayer asking God to change each person's life.

Midweek program

For a more informal midweek setting, use more of the hands-on activities and games that are suggested as responses to the story. It is crucial, however, that the Bible story continues to be the central focus of the event. Many of the ideas suggested for Sunday school are appropriate for the midweek programme.

All-church worship—education event

Invite the entire congregation to participate in this already broadly graded curriculum. Young and old can learn from each other by doing and experiencing the friendship of Jesus. For an integrated two-hour worship and education event, develop one of the session themes. Sessions one, two, or five would be particularly appropriate for an intergenerational event.

Begin the session with approximately thirty minutes of worship. Sing the songs, present the Bible story drama as the day's message, and include the other necessary elements of worship.

For the next hour, invite multi-age groupings of up to ten people to participate in one workshop. Workshops can be based on the Then and Now, Make and Take, Games and Snacks, Early Childhood, and Junior Youth sections of the curriculum. Add other workshop ideas. In each workshop the group reviews the story, makes the connection of the story with the activity, participates in the activity, and shares personal responses through discussion, debriefing, and prayer.

The entire group reassembles after the workshop time for closing songs and a benediction. A celebration meal would make a great ending to this all-church worship event.

All-church weekend programme

Some churches enjoy a camping weekend. This curriculum would provide excellent resource material for a weekend vacation Bible school programme for the entire congregation. Use the five sessions as outlined in the curriculum. A drama group can be practising for the next session while the other participants are engaged in response activities. Divide the group into multi-age groupings and have each group rotate to Make and Take, Then and Now, Games and Snacks, or allow individuals to choose activities in which they wish to participate. Find different leaders for each response session. If the leadership is shared among youth, young adults, and adults, preparation is at a minimum, and everyone can have a good time together all weekend.

Camping program

The out-of-doors would provide a wonderful setting for stories about Peter to come alive. What better place to experience the story of Peter's call from fisherman to follower than beside a lake! Most of the activities would work well out-of-doors. Staff as well as campers will find this programme exciting and energizing. Set up centres for rotation by groups. Each child participates in each event every day. The staff person or leader presents the same material to each group.

Family vacation time

Some families spend several weeks at a summer cottage or traveling during the summer months. Take *Simon Peter* along on vacation for your family worship time. Read the stories or act them out together. Family members can choose which response activities to do together from the age-appropriate categories listed in each section.

Parents and grandparents could use this curriculum as they care for their children and the neighbour's children during those lazy, hazy days of summer or any time throughout the year.

Get It Organized

Leaders and responsibilities

Coordinator

- Supervises the entire program.
- Works with a committee to find leaders.
- Distributes curriculum and supplies to the other leaders. Be sure Group leaders have copies of the the resources listed on page 17.
- Decides on an offering project.
- Looks after promotion and publicity, registration, and attendance details.

Registration

As the children arrive on the first day, assign them to their small group. Lists of pre-registered children could be prepared beforehand to speed up registration. You may hand out the prepared name tags or have the children put their names on the tags themselves. If you have a large group to register, set up tables according to the ages of the children. As children arrive, send them to the appropriate table for a name tag and group assignment. If the groups are broadly graded (kindergarten-grade 5), it is best to have each child with one other person she or he knows.

Bible story drama coordinator

- Supervises the daily Bible story dramas. Some drama experience and skills are helpful, but not necessary.
- Coordinates the people or team who present the Bible story dramas. See Worship Resource, pages 31-60.

Bible story presenters

(Five or more people with some acting abilities)
- Present the daily Bible story dramas effectively. See pages 34-49.

Music coordinator

- Chooses the songs that are appropriate to the theme, age level, interests, and abilities of the children. Learn and be prepared to teach a theme song.

"Hallelujah Ballad—Peter," page 51, is recommended.
- Finds people to lead and/or accompany the singing. See Worship Resource, pages 31-60.

Worship leader
- Coordinates the worship time with the Bible story presenters and music personnel.
- Introduces the theme and story each day.
- Is responsible for announcements, dismissal to activities, etc. See Worship Resource, pages 31-60.

Then and Now leader
- Has good communication skills with children, enjoys memory work, has an interest in drama, can stimulate discussion.
- Can solicit the active participation of Group leaders to help with small group activities.
- Is well organized and prepares ahead of time.

Make and Take leader
- Enjoys being creative with hands-on materials.
- Encourages children to be creative as they make something that reflects their personal understanding of the daily theme.
- Helps children express themselves in their own way. Does not insist on uniform, perfect creations by the children but sees the craft activity as a time for self-expression.
- Engages the Group leaders as willing assistants and full participants in the activity.
- Makes application of the activity to the theme of the day.

Games leader
- Enjoys leading and participating in active games.
- Has good communication skills with children, likes to play, and has the ability to make applications of the games to the theme of the day.
- Works with the Snacks coordinator so that snacks arrive at the appropriate time without disrupting the group.
- Can solicit the active participation of Group leaders to help with the games. Gives Group leaders clear instructions and assignments and expects them to participate fully in all activities.

Snacks coordinator
Organizes the snacks for each day. (See page 82 for ideas. Games and Snacks, pages 81-96, gives suggestions on how to integrate the snacks into the activities.) If the rotation system is used, it is best to serve the snacks at the end of the session for the first group and at the beginning of the session for the second and third groups.

Group leaders

- Enjoy children. Act as friends and positive role models. Be good listeners. Be accepting and responsible.
- Early Childhood Group leaders, see page 114 for a description of your responsibilities.
- Junior Youth leaders, see page 162 for your responsibilities.
- Kindergarten to grade 5 Group leaders, see pages 14-17 for your responsibilities.

Introduction

As a Group leader, you are a very important person in this programme. You could compare yourself to a counsellor at camp, one who spends quality time with children. You are the adult who will spend the most time with the children in your group. You have the great opportunity and privilege to become a special friend and role model to the children. You are the one who will demonstrate to them what it means to follow Jesus as a grown-up. You are the one who can model Jesus' loving care to each child in your group.

Although you are not involved in the major part of the planning, you are responsible for community building among group members, for making each child feel accepted and welcome, and for seeing that the children cooperate and participate in the variety of activities each day.

Group leaders care about children and about God. To be effective, you need to enjoy children, to relate easily to children from a variety of homes and backgrounds, and to accept each child as a person loved by God. Be a leader who is nonjudgmental, a good listener, responsible, and eager to make this time together with the children a positive, transforming experience for yourself and for each child.

Responsibilities

You are responsible for knowing what is happening in all areas of the programme that affect you as a Group leader. Ask the coordinator to see the introductory materials, pages 6-8; 14-22, including the Master Schedule. Read through this information carefully, noting areas that affect you.

Registration and name tags

1. Prepare name tags for your group members. Have available markers for them to put their names on the name tags.

2. Have registration forms (page 27) ready for distribution at the end of the first day. Ask the coordinator for these forms.

3. Provide a container for the offering.

4. Prepare the attendance record (see page 29) if desired. If you are using names of fish for your groups, prepare a paper fishbowl for each child. Have each child cut out a fish picture from a magazine, draw a fish, or place a fish sticker onto the fishbowl each day. If you are using rock names, have a collection of stones on hand. Each day the children may choose a stone and glue it onto the previous day's stone to form a rock sculpture. If you do this activity, help the children with the hot glue gun.

Gather and Greet

1. Make your gathering place a welcoming place for your group. Whether you meet in a classroom, tent, or on a blanket out-of-doors, do whatever you can to help the children feel comfortable and at home. Decorate the area using the theme of fish and/or rocks. Have a display of books, rocks, and polished stones. To illustrate the transformation theme, set up a terrarium, plant a fast-growing bulb or seed, or display a cocoon and butterfly. Have a magnifying glass or stool available for children to get a close-up view of changing life.

2. Arrive early to greet and welcome each child by name. As the children arrive, they can look at books, check living things through a magnifying glass, or help with name tags and attendance. They can place their offering in the container.

3. When everyone is present, sit in a circle to learn each other's name. Begin by going around the circle and having everyone say her or his name. After each name is given, everyone should repeat it together. Continue around the circle a second time, having everyone give the name of the person on her or his right. Again, have everyone repeat the name together. Do this again to the left of the person. Next, go around the circle with the entire group shouting each person's name.

4. Explain your daily ritual to the children–how you wish to begin each day in your group. Explain about name tags, attendance, pre-session activities, and offering.

5. Before you move to Worship, invite the children to pray with you. Offer a simple prayer, inviting God to be present with each person and with the group as together you learn about Simon Peter and his friendship with Jesus.

6. Go together to Worship.

Worship

Sit with your group and participate in the songs and motions you are asked to do. Remember that you are modelling acceptable behaviour for the children. When you become actively involved, the children will also participate. It is your responsibility to manage undesirable behaviour. Sit beside a fidgety, noisy child. If the child becomes distracting, do not hesitate to remove that child from the assembly area until she or he is ready to sit quietly. Listen carefully for instructions regarding the rotation to activities, etc., before dismissal.

Then and Now

1. Accompany your group to the Then and Now meeting place. Be a willing participant. You are the Then and Now leader's assistant. Be prepared to help as you are directed. Ask the resource leader beforehand how she or he expects you to help.

2. Learn the memory text (2 Peter 1:3, 5-7) along with the children. The memory text is printed on pages 63-64.

3. Involve yourself in the Bible story dramas and help the children retell the story with your encouragement and enthusiasm. Talk with your group about Peter and his relationship with Jesus. Be willing to tell the group about your personal relationship with Jesus. Jesus can become a real friend for the children as they see that you take your relationship with him seriously and are comfortable talking about it. Listen to what the children say and build on their thoughts. Do not force your adult views on them. Let the Holy Spirit

guide the discussion.

4. Keep an eye on the clock. Help the Then and Now leader clean up and prepare for the next group. Go with your group to the next activity.

Games and Snacks

If possible, spend this time out-of-doors. Depending upon the rotation, you may begin with the snack. Be prepared to serve the snack to your group and help them with it. Offer your assistance to the Games leader and plan to become actively involved. Children usually enjoy when the adults are having fun with them. Participate and enjoy!

Make and Take

Accompany your group to the craft meeting place and offer to assist the Make and Take leader in any way. Again, be prepared to do as instructed, and help the children who require assistance. Help with the cleanup and preparation for the next group. Lead your group to the next activity.

Gather and Bless

1. Closing time will take place either in the large assembly group or within the small groups. Learn the closing blessing song, "One in Love," with the hand motions beforehand (see pages 52-53). Help the children learn the song and motions.

If you have a younger group of children, teach the song and have your group decide on appropriate motions for the words.

2. Take time to review the day. Ask the children to tell what they liked best, what they did not especially like, what the Bible story was about, and what one thing they will tell their parents about God. Sit in a circle for this time of sharing. Have a group prayer or review the memory text. Close with the blessing.

3. Give announcements and reminders to the children. Distribute any materials that need to go home. See that the children have their crafts to take home.

4. Collect the name tags. Encourage the children to come back and bring a friend.

Additional group-building ideas

1. Develop a group cheer. Use your group name and make a rhyming poem or a short catchy song that describes who you are.

2. Learn about each other's favourite things. Give each person the opportunity to tell the group what is her or his favourite snack food, dessert, television show, colour, vacation spot, book, or Bible story.

3. Learn about each child's family. Do a family "sculpture." Each child should place the other group members in some position that illustrates his or her household: brothers, sisters, parents, relatives, boarders. Then explain the sculpture. Where does the person fit in the family order? What would the child like to say about her or his family?

4. Introduce each session's theme with a related activity.

- Session 1: Learn everyone's name. Play a game such as a ball toss to help the children repeat and remember each other's name.
- Session 2: Have a very short trust walk. Join hands and lead the group on a short walk, perhaps with a few obstacles to avoid by stepping over or around them. Then repeat the walk with the children joining hands but

without your hand to guide them. Guide them along the same course by giving verbal instructions. Talk about the meaning of trust.

- Session 3: Talk about friendships. Who is the child's best friend? What makes a best friend? How does one make new friends? How does one feel when let down by a friend?
- Session 4: Invite each child to mime different ways to celebrate. Practise facial expressions of joy and celebration. Form a tableau by "freezing" the expression on signal.
- Session 5: Celebrate your last day together with an affirmation exercise. Form a circle. Ask for a volunteer to step into the circle. Invite the other children to complete this sentence, "I am glad you were in our group because. . . ." Allow time for everyone to be affirmed.

Personal preparation

To prepare yourself for this important ministry, spend time in prayer for the programme, the leaders, and your role. Study the Bible. Read the biblical texts for each day's story and reflect on them from your personal experience. (These themes are listed on page 7.) Ask the Holy Spirit to give you new insights on the Scriptures and on the life of Simon Peter. Consider the faith focus for each day. How do you respond to the text? How will you respond to God's call to you to be a faithful disciple of Jesus Christ?

Resources

Ask your Coordinator for the following resources:
Session titles and themes, pages 19-20;
Master Schedule, page 22;
Registration Form, page 27;
Attendance Form, page 29;
Closing Blessing, pages 52-53;
Memory text (2 Peter 1:3, 5-7 NRSV), pages 63-64.

Know the children

If you teach a broadly graded group (kindergarten to grade 5)

- Respect each child as an individual with special needs and gifts.
- Remember the broader age span and use appropriate language in your discussions and teaching.
- Encourage children to respond at their individual level of understanding.
- Encourage the active participation of each person.
- Promote group building and learning across the ages by pairing up older and younger children for discussion and activity and by forming small groups that include people of each age group for games, skits, crafts, etc.

If you teach early childhood

- Demonstrate a love for young children.
- Have patience.
- Be well organized and plan ahead so that the children are cared for all the time.

Early childhood sessions are built around the same themes as those for older children. However, early childhood should hold their sessions independently. Directions for getting the early childhood programme organized are found on pages 114-116 in the Early Childhood section.

If you teach primary children

Children in kindergarten through grade 2 think of God as a friend to whom they can talk. They have not yet developed abstract reasoning. They are usually trusting of adults. Use their spiritual understanding and provide caring and loving models that they can trust and follow. Remember that they have limited reading ability and learn best by doing and seeing.

If you teach middler children

Children in the middle grades are beginning to develop abstract thinking. They have a strong sense of fairness, of right and wrong. Be sure that you present the biblical concepts of God's forgiveness, of God's love and care for everyone. Model God's forgiveness and have concern for others. Include all the children in activities that meet their needs. Value their questions and invite them to a loving relationship with Jesus who taught us how to live God's way.

If you teach junior youth

- Enjoy being with adolescents.
- Serve as an active listener, a discussion facilitator, a person who cares about the natural and spiritual development of the young adolescents.
- Be an advocate for the junior youth, intent on helping them to grow into a loving relationship with Jesus.
- Model a positive relationship with Jesus and be willing to talk about it with young people.
- Invite youth to ask their faith questions and do not insist on giving them the answers.
- Be willing to adapt the curriculum to the needs of the children in your care.

Session titles and themes

Session 1

An Invitation to Follow

Theme: From Fisherman to Follower
Bible Text: Mark 1:16-20; Luke 5:1-11
Biblical Background: Mark 1:1-31
Story Focus: Peter was a fisherman who chose to give up his nets and his job to become a follower of Jesus. This was the beginning of a relationship with Jesus that would change his entire life.
Faith Focus: Jesus invites us to become his followers for life.

Session 2

An Invitation to Faith

Theme: From Faith to Failure to Faith
Bible Text: Matthew 14:22-33
Story Focus: Peter's initial faith in Jesus faltered when he attempted to walk on the water to meet Jesus. After Jesus rescued him, Peter and the disciples believed that Jesus was God's special son.
Faith Focus: When we focus on Jesus, we can do more than we think we can.

Session 3

An Invitation to Loyalty

Theme: From Loyalty to Betrayal
Bible Texts: John 13:34-38; Mark 14:66-72
Biblical Background: John 13:1-38; John 18:1-11; Luke 22:51; John 19:1–20:23
Story Focus: Peter wanted to be a loyal friend to Jesus, but when frightening things that he did not understand began to happen, he denied the friendship. Even though Peter did not pass the loyalty test, Jesus continued to love him.
Faith Focus: It is easy to slip back into old patterns of behaviour when we are faced with new and frightening situations. Jesus continues to love and forgive us even when we do not act like his friend.

Session 4

An Invitation to Courage

Theme: From Fear to Courage
Bible Text: Acts 2:1-42
Story Focus: At Pentecost, God's Spirit changed Peter from a fearful follower to a courageous leader. Peter was no longer afraid to tell others about Jesus when he realized that the Holy Spirit was helping him.
Faith Focus: When we let God's Holy Spirit live in us, we are given courage to act boldly for Jesus.

Session 5

An Invitation to Acceptance

Theme: From Rejection to Acceptance
Bible Text: Acts 10:1-48
Story Focus: After a vision from God, Peter believed that it was not right for him to be prejudiced against people who were not Jews. All people are equally accepted by God.
Faith Focus: When we think like God, we value all people as God does.

Schedule

	Session Titles	Themes
Session 1	An Invitation to Follow	From Fisherman to Follower
Session 2	An Invitation to Faith	From Faith to Failure to Faith
Session 3	An Invitation to Loyalty	From Loyalty to Betrayal
Session 4	An Invitation to Courage	From Fear to Courage
Session 5	An Invitation to Acceptance	From Rejection to Acceptance

The memory text is 2 Peter 1:3, 5-7 (NRSV). Children will be invited to learn this text in the Then and Now time. The text is printed on pages 63-64.

Gather and Greet (15 minutes)

Small groups meet with the group leaders for attendance, offering, morning prayer, and group-building activities. Meet in the same place every day—in a classroom, on a blanket outside, or in an auditorium. The Group leader interacts informally with the children, welcomes them to the day's activities, and engages them in simple activities that will help the group begin to feel like a community. Pick a group name to identify yourself. Go together to the assembly area for Worship.

Worship (30 minutes)

Children from kindergarten to grade 8 meet in an assembly area to sing songs and watch the Bible story drama. Begin the worship with familiar "sing-along" songs that are favourites of the children. Songs that fit the general theme, as well as songs that are more specific to the daily focus, are included for each day. The music can be found on pages 51-60.

Story is a powerful method of sharing truth with children of all ages. Five stories in the form of drama tell about Peter and his growing relationship with God. The dramas are written for five characters. For more details about characters, costumes, setting and props, see Worship Resource, pages 32-33. It is recommended that you have a drama group prepare and present all five dramas so that the characters can be consistent and more fully developed.

Prepare a focal point for worship. Use a large wooden cross. Each day add a different symbol on the cross, e.g. fishing nets, boat sail, flame-coloured headbands, a sheet with stuffed animals.

Activity time (105 minutes)

There is a three-way rotation of activity. After Worship, each group is sent to one of the three activity centres—Then and Now, Games and Snacks, and

Make and Take–for a thirty-minute session. Five minutes are allowed for travel time between centres. Each group will rotate to each centre each session. Vary the rotation so that the groups will start at a different centre some days. If groups need to be combined for the rotation, be sure to put different groups together each day. Set up a chart similar to the one below to show the rotation each day.

Three-way Rotation Plan

Up to 30 children (3 groups)

Session 1	Then and Now	Games and Snack	Make and Take
Rotation 1 9:45 - 10:15	Group 1	Group 2	Group 3
Rotation 2 10:15 - 10:45	Group 2	Group 3	Group 1
Rotation 3 10:45 - 11:15	Group 3	Group 1	Group 2

Up to 60 (double groups—2 per rotation)

Session 1	Then and Now	Games and Snack	Make and Take
Rotation 1 9:45 - 10:15	Groups 1, 2	Groups 3, 4	Groups 5, 6
Rotation 2 10:15 - 10:45	Groups 3, 4	Groups 5, 6	Groups 1, 2
Rotation 3 10:45 - 11:15	Groups 5, 6	Groups 1, 2	Groups 3, 4

Up to 90 children (triple groups—3 per rotation)

Session 1	Then and Now	Games and Snack	Make and Take
Rotation 1 9:45 - 10:15	Groups 1, 2, 3	Groups 4, 5, 6	Groups 7, 8, 9
Rotation 2 10:15 - 10:45	Groups 4, 5, 6	Groups 7, 8, 9	Groups 1, 2, 3
Rotation 3 10:45 - 11:15	Groups 7, 8, 9	Groups 1, 2, 3	Groups 4, 5, 6

If you have more than 90, add a second complete rotation schedule.

Master Schedule

9:00 - 9:15 GATHER AND GREET (Meet in small groups for attendance, offering, group building)					

9:15 - 9:45 WORSHIP (Total group assembly)					
Themes and Bible Texts	Session 1 *Invitation to Follow* Peter: From Fisherman to Follower Mark 1:16-20; Luke 5:1-11	Session 2 *Invitation to Faith* Peter: From Faith to Failure to Faith Matthew 14:22-33	Session 3 *Invitation to Loyalty* Peter: From Loyalty to Betrayal John 13:34-38; Mark 14:66-72	Session 4 *Invitation to Courage* Peter: From Fear to Courage Acts 2:1-42	Session 5 *Invitation to Acceptance* Peter: From Rejection to Acceptance Acts 10:1-48

9:45 -11:15 THREE-WAY ROTATION ACTIVITY TIME (Kindergarten - Grade 5)					
35 Minutes **THEN AND NOW** Review, respond, remember	Memory work THEN - review story through creative drama NOW - invitation to follow activity	Memory work THEN - review story with accordion booklet NOW - sharing about difficult things to do	Memory work THEN - review story with clay characters NOW - stories about friendship	Memory work THEN - review story with sounds and streamers NOW - facing our fears discussion	Memory work THEN - review story through discussion NOW - role-plays
35 Minutes **GAMES AND SNACKS**	• Rock Call • Crazy Relay • Human Fish • Rock, Paper Scissors	• Stepping Stones • Waves in the Water • Rock Tag	• Bubble Over • Ten-legged Race • Blanket Ball Toss • Partner Activities	• Frozen Tag • Spread the Spirit • Watch for the Spirit • Prisoner's Base	**Cultural Games** • Freeze • Chopstick Relay • Bucket Brigade • Stone Catch
35 Minutes **MAKE AND TAKE**	• Pet Rocks or • Rock Paperweight	• Sinking Peter Puppet • Terrarium	• Pliers • Friendship Cards • Friendship Pennant or Place Mat	• Holy Spirit Mobile • Wind Chimes	• Butterfly or • Fish

11:15 - 11:30 GATHER AND BLESS (Meet as a larger assembly or in small groups for reviewing memory work and songs. Close with the blessing, "One in Love.")					

EARLY CHILDHOOD (ages 3, 4, and 5)   Each session includes: The same Bible story written as a simple story, Bible story reenactment, talk time, an activity page for an accordion book, a craft, games, snack, puppet play, and closing blessing.

JUNIOR YOUTH (grades 6-8) Junior youth form a separate group for **Gather and Greet** and during the 105-minute rotation. During the rotation time, there will be a Bible study and suggestions for responding to the Bible story through crafts, games, service project, reflection, etc.

Permission is granted to photocopy this Master Schedule.

Leader options

If you teach the complete session for one age
- Early Childhood: Use the Early Childhood section, pages 113-159.
- Kindergarten-grade 2: Use the daily session plans for Gather and Greet, Worship, Then and Now, Games and Snacks, Make and Take, and Gather and Bless from each of these Resource sections.
- Grades 3-5: Use the daily session plans for Gather and Greet, Worship, Then and Now, Games and Snacks, Make and Take, and Gather and Bless from each of these Resource sections.
- Grades 6-8: Use the Junior Youth section, pages 161-195.
  Follow the three-way rotation plan with your individual grade.

If you teach or lead Worship, Then and Now, Games and Snacks, or Make and Take
- Follow the daily session plans in your corresponding resource section. See the Table of Contents.

Set up a three-way rotation for kindergarten-grade 5
(This plan works best with three equal groups of equal numbers, up to 30 in each group.)
- See the Three-way Rotation Plan, page 21. Change the rotation pattern each day.

Then and Now (30 minutes)
Reinforce the Bible story with the children. Use creative drama, the arts, play dough, etc., to help the children re-enact the story and talk about its meaning for them. Suggestions for discussion and modern-day stories that relate to the daily themes are included.

Children will work together to learn the memory text. Each day, the teacher will use a creative learning device to help the children memorize 2 Peter 1:3, 5-7.

See page 62 for Then and Now leader responsibilities.

Games and Snacks (30 minutes)
Use this time for active learning. The games and physical activities reinforce the daily themes and encourage community building among group members. Snack time is also included.

See page 83 for Games leader and Snack coordinator responsibilities.

Make and Take (30 minutes)
Reinforce the theme through craft and creative arts activities. See page 98 for Make and Take leader responsibilities.

Gather and Bless (15 minutes)

Gather again in an assembly group or as small groups to review the day's theme, sing the theme songs, review the memory work, and make any announcements. Close with the blessing "One in Love," pages 52-53. Create your own symbolic movements for the words. Teach the song to the whole group on the first day.

See page 16 for Group leader responsibilities.

Age/grade groupings

Early Childhood

Children ages three, four, and five participate in the early childhood programme. The children are placed in groups with an adult leader. They do not need to be separated by ages. See Early Childhood, pages 113-159, for complete session plans.

Kindergarten - grade 5

Children who have completed kindergarten through grade 5 make up the second group of children. Form them into small groups made up of one adult and no more than ten children. Groups can be broadly graded by having two children of each age in each group, or by dividing children into younger (Kindergarten, 1, 2) and older (3, 4, 5) groups.

Junior Youth

Children who have completed grades 6, 7, and 8 form a separate group for part of the programme. This group remains together regardless of size. However, have an adult Group leader for each group of ten participants. See the Junior Youth section, pages 161-195. Junior youth participate as a separate group for Gather and Greet and during the rotation activities. Each day during the rotation period (105 minutes), junior youth will have their own Bible study and response time. Junior youth participate with kindergarten - grade 5 for Worship and may or may not be part of the Gather and Greet.

Additional helps

Extra group names

Choose names that will be easy to identify, pronounce, and understand. It would be appropriate to use names of fish, since the logo is a fish. Simon Peter was a fisherman by trade, and the fish symbol was used by the early church as a secret sign for Christians. You might also use the Group leader's name for additional identification, e.g., "Susan's Sunfish," "Dan's Dolphins." Here are some fish names from which to choose:

bass	dolphin
trout	halibut
sunfish	pickerel
perch	haddock
salmon	goldfish

Names of precious gemstones would also be appropriate. Peter is referred to as "rock" by Jesus.

diamond	gold	silver
opal	emerald	aquamarine
sapphire	coral	platinum

Name tags

If fish names are being used, have Group leaders make name tags in the shape of their chosen or assigned fish out of construction paper or bristol board. Punch a hole in the top of the tag and string a piece of coloured yarn through so that the tag can be worn around the neck. You may wish to use safety pins to attach to the child's clothing. To lengthen the life of the name tag, you can cover it with adhesive-backed clear plastic. The tags are handed in to the Group leader at the end of each session. Encourage Group leaders to call each child by name as much as possible.

Snack suggestions

Choose snacks that are easy to prepare and that the children will enjoy. If possible, have a Snack coordinator to work with the Games leader. This person will prepare snacks and deliver them to each group at the appropriate times. Nutritious snacks include:

- Cookies with whole grain or wheat flour
- Apple slices with peanut butter
- Celery sticks with a cheese spread
- Gorp (good old raisins and peanuts)
- Nuts
- Pretzels
- Fresh fruits and vegetables
- Popcorn (Session 5)

Closing celebration

A closing assembly has many useful purposes. Parents are given the opportunity to meet the Group leaders and teachers. Many parents like to know what is being taught to their children in Christian education. Encourage the leaders to talk about the curriculum and their children's evaluation of it.

Leaders have the privilege of meeting and greeting the parents of the children they have had in their care. Use this informal time to invite new families to continue to be a part of your worshiping community.

This assembly is meant to be an informal gathering time for children, leaders, and parents and not a polished performance by the children.

Include some of the following in your celebrations:
1. Sing the theme songs and other favourites.
2. Repeat the memory text together.
3. Review the stories using the cross and daily symbols.
4. Display some of the crafts and art activities.
5. Show video clips of some of the activities (pre-recorded).
6. Share a simple snack.
7. Close with the "One in Love" blessing.

Logo

The curved shape of the letters suggest that Peter's character is changing because of his relationship to Jesus. The "t" in Peter's name is symbolic of the cross. As followers of Jesus we recognize the importance of Jesus' death and resurrection and his power to transform our lives.

The fish was the secret symbol used by first-century Christians to identify themselves as followers of Jesus. People would mark the symbol in the dirt with a sandal or stick so that others would know with whom it was safe to talk about Jesus or where to meet secretly for worship. The Greek word for fish is pronounced "ichthus" and is an acrostic containing the first letter, in Greek, of each of these words: Jesus, Christ, God's, Son, Saviour.

Registration Form

Please complete this form and give it to the Group leader by _____ .

Name of child _____

Address _____

Telephone _____

Birth date _____
        (month)   (day)   (year)

Last school grade completed _____

Known allergies or other medical concerns _____

_____

Name of parent/primary caregiver _____

Home telephone _____

Work telephone _____

Emergency contact person _____

Emergency telephone _____

Does the child usually attend Sunday school? _____

If so, where? _____

WAIVER OF RESPONSIBILITY

I give _____ permission to participate in this
                    (child's name)
programme. The leaders will not be held responsible for injury, etc.

Parent/guardian signature _____

Date _____

Permission is granted to photocopy this page.

SIMON PETER GROUP ASSIGNMENT FORM

	NAME	AGE	GRADE	GROUP ASSIGNED	COMMENT

Permission is granted to photocopy this page.

SIMON PETER ATTENDANCE FORM

GROUP_____

LEADERS _____

NAME	SESSION 1	SESSION 2	SESSION 3	SESSION 4	SESSION 5	COMMENT
1.						
2.						
3.						
4.						
5.						
6.						
7.						
8.						
9.						
10.						
11.						
12.						
13.						
14.						
15.						
16.						
17.						
18.						
19.						
20.						

Permission is granted to photocopy this page.

Permission is granted to photocopy this page.

Worship
Resource

Worship Resource

Introduction

Music

Appropriate music, including the theme song, "Hallelujah Ballad–Peter," is printed on page 51. Use these songs and other favourites during Worship. Make Worship a time to praise and celebrate God's presence in your lives.

Bible stories

The Bible stories are written in dramatic form. Read all the dramas to understand the character of Peter and the other characters. Study the biblical texts and background material for each session to understand the main focus for the story.

Characters

Each drama includes five characters. Peter and Jesus or the Holy Spirit appear in every drama. The other three characters include narrators, disciples, a tableau/mime group, and an army officer.

It is recommended that you invite five people to form a drama troupe that will prepare and present all five dramas. Consistent character development of Peter, the main person in the story, is important. Peter is being transformed each day into the likeness of Jesus, the one whom he has chosen to follow. Children can identify better with one person playing the role of Peter. If possible, the Peter and Jesus characters should be played by men. Women can play the parts of disciples, the Spirit, and the other characters.

If it is not possible to have Peter and Jesus played by men, make face masks that have masculine features. Craft supply stores have materials to form masks. Purchase a package of Rigid-Wrap. Follow instructions which apply to using it on the skin and form a mask from the face of the people who will play these characters. When the masks are dry, add masculine features, such as beards or mustaches.

Using masks for all of the main characters will prevent young children from becoming confused with the identity of the people in the drama troupe whom they may know.

Costuming

Find simple clothing in the loose-fitting style of male dress during the first century. Lightweight brown or dark bathrobes tied at the waist work well. The fishermen should have bare feet or wear thongs or sandals.

For Session 4, the Holy Spirit appears as a character. The Spirit is portrayed as a person whom Peter can see but the disciples cannot see. Dress the character portraying the Holy Spirit in a yellow or orange outfit. Brilliant colours work best. A black or red Spirit could give a negative image of God; a white image may be too ghostlike.

Staging

Use an area that everyone can see for the stage. You may be as elaborate as you wish. The only prop necessary is a large wooden cross set on the stage. Each session attach a different symbol to the cross to represent the theme: Session 1, a fishing net; Session 2, a boat sail; Session 4, a number of flame-coloured headbands; Session 5, a bed sheet with stuffed toys. In Session 3, the cross remains bare to symbolize Peter's betrayal and the death of Jesus on the cross.

Add other props appropriate to the setting: Sessions 1 and 2, a real or cardboard boat, nets, fish, and a sail; Session 2, oars for rowing; Session 4, simple furniture.

Invite artistic adults and carpenters to design the staging. Involve adults in the programme who have never participated in vacation Bible school.

Presentation of the Bible dramas

Memorize and rehearse each drama. These stories are the basis for all the activities in the session programme. If the stories are well presented, children will be able to identify with Peter and understand what it is like to be a follower of Jesus and to accept the leading of the Holy Spirit.

If there are many younger children in the programme, have Peter and the disciples put on their costumes on the stage while the drama is being introduced. Watching this preparation will help the children know that it is time for the Bible story and that the adults are acting in the role of biblical characters.

Make the Bible story presentation educational and engaging to the children and adults. Let God's message of transforming love to humanity be expressed in the stories as they are dramatized.

Involving junior youth

If you have a junior youth group (grades 6, 7, 8), ask them to participate in the Session 2 drama as the "Weather Chorus," Session 4 as the crowd, and in Session 5 as Cornelius's family. Allow for some rehearsal time during the junior youth separate session on the day before the drama is being presented.

Session plans
Bible stories and dramas

Session 1

An Invitation to Follow

> **Theme:** From Fisherman to Follower
> **Bible Text:** Mark 1:16-20; Luke 5:1-11
> **Biblical Background:** Mark 1:1-31
> **Story Focus:** Peter was a fisherman who chose to give up his nets and his job to become a follower of Jesus. This was the beginning of a relationship with Jesus that would change his entire life.
> **Faith Focus:** Jesus invites us to become his followers for life.

Anticipated Outcomes

1. The children are introduced to the characters of Jesus and Peter and the beginning of a friendship between the two men. They will learn that Jesus invited Peter and his brother, Andrew, who were ordinary fishermen to become his followers. Without hesitation, they left their fishing nets and became Jesus' disciples.

2. The children will be introduced to the concept that following Jesus means a change in attitudes, behaviour, and character.

Materials

- A large simple wooden cross
- A net draped over the cross (use a volleyball net or a hammock)
- Other props as desired: a boat, oars, fishing nets, pails, rope
- Costumes for Simon, Jesus, Andrew, and the children

Worship

Sings songs on pages 51-60 and other favourites. Teach the theme song, "Hallelujah Ballad–Peter," page 51. Pray.

Introduction

The drama can be introduced either by one of the drama troupe members or by the Worship leader. Characters put on their costumes and prepare for the drama.

Leader: This week we will be learning about a man named Simon Peter. Simon Peter lived a long time ago, in the first century, at the time when Jesus lived on the earth. The story today tells how Simon and his brother, Andrew, met Jesus. A close friendship between Simon and Jesus began. Because of this friendship, Simon Peter changed as a person. Every day we will see a change in him, sometimes for the better and sometimes for the worse. I hope you will come back every day to find out how Peter changed because of his friendship with Jesus. Right now, let's pay attention to the story, called "The Meeting."

Present the Bible story drama, "The Meeting."

Dismissal

Without discussing the story, send the children to the next activity where they will have the opportunity to respond to the story in appropriate ways. Make sure that each Group leader knows the order of rotation to Then and Now, Games and Snacks, and Make and Take activities.

THE MEETING

Cast: Narrator, Child, Simon (Peter), Jesus, Andrew

The narrator may involve a small crowd of children who "hang out" with her or him.

Setting: *The seashore may have some large "rocks" on which the children sit. Simon and Andrew are in the background netting bait. Use a real or imaginary boat and other fishing props. The cross is draped with nets.*

Narrator: We children love to play here on the beach. Sometimes we talk or fight or just soak up the welcome winter sun. The rough limestone ridge rises in a broken wall along the beach. There are many little sunny nooks protected from the wind.

There is always something to see. James and John are working on their nets. They spread the nets out on the large flat rocks just above the water line to pick out twigs and seaweed and to check for weak or worn places. Sometimes we bigger kids can earn a wedge of barley bread or a dried fig by helping unload the boats or washing them out with water scooped from the lake in leather buckets.

Simon and Andrew are netting bait in the shallows. I like Simon best. He moved to Capernaum with his family a few years ago. He works hard and yells a lot. He and his brother became partners with James and John whose family has fished these waters longer than anyone can remember. He often tells stories of terrifying storms or monster fish that get bigger every time he repeats the stories. But it is always his own strength and courage that save the day. The more exciting his stories get, the louder the other fishermen chuckle and the more furiously he glares at them from beneath his frightening, thick eyebrows.

Sometimes he is too busy for stories. If we get too close, he yells terrible threats and flails at us with a length of rope. He never carries out the threats, and the rope never hits anything but the gravelly beach. At other times he tells us to move back and gives us strips of tangy dried fish from his wife's mother. Everyone wants a piece of her fish. People come from far away for a taste of it. We children like Simon in spite of his temper and scary looks.

Child: Look! Who is that coming up the beach?

Narrator: Oh, I know him. That's Jesus, the woodworker from Nazareth. He fixed our door after the storm last week.

[*Enter Jesus, who stops by Peter and Andrew.*]

He went to the synagogue with all the men last Sabbath and got everybody excited by healing a man who had a demon. Then he went to Simon's house and healed his wife's mother who almost died of a fever. Everyone's been talking about him all week. I wonder what they are saying now.

Simon: I know I owe you for healing my mother-in-law, but you are wasting our time. We have been fishing all night, and I'm tired. There's nothing out there.

Jesus: Let's go out just one more time. I hear you are the best fishermen in the area.

Simon: Well, that's the truth, but no one can make the fish jump into the boat when they don't want to.

Andrew: Come on, Simon. We have no fish to clean or take to the market, so what harm can it do?

Simon: Oh, all right. But I know these waters, and I still say we are wasting our time.

[*Jesus, Simon, and Andrew enter boat. Simon and Andrew row.*]

Jesus: Stop right aboouuut . . . here!

Andrew: This is not a good place.

Simon: We've never caught anything here, ever!

Jesus: Just let down your net.

[*Peter shrugs and rolls his eyes.*]

Andrew: Let's give it a try. What can we lose?

[*They lower the net.*]

Simon: [*Muttering*] Don't say I didn't warn you. I bet we're going to lose the net on top of everything else. I haven't even had a decent meal since yesterday. I'm just sick and tired of all this . . . this . . . (tugs at the net, which won't budge). What the. . . !

Andrew: Look at all those fish!

Simon: Easy now! Drop it back into the water before the net breaks. Call James and John to come and help us.

[*Both call loudly, lifting up imaginary fish from the net into the boat.*]

Andrew: Wow! Any more fish and this boat is going to sink!

Simon: [*Falling on his knees*] Lord, keep away from me! I am a sinful person.

Jesus: I know. Don't worry, we're going to be working on that. But from now on you are going to be catching people. And I am going to help you, just as I did with the fish.

Simon: What do you mean by "catching people," Lord?

Jesus: You, Simon, are going to help me gather a group of people to be my faithful helpers. To remind you of the kind of people I want and the kind of person I want you to become, I am giving you a new name. From now on you are no longer Simon. You will be known as Peter.

Simon: Peter!?

Andrew: Yes, I get it. Peter means . . . uh . . . rock, doesn't it?

Peter: Peter, rock. Rock, Peter. Yes. Rock-solid Peter. I like it. I can live with that.

Jesus: Now then, just leave everything here, come and follow me.

[*Peter and Andrew follow Jesus as they exit together.*]

Permission is granted to photocopy pages 35 and 36 for drama presenters.

Session 2

An Invitation to Faith

Theme: From Faith to Failure to Faith
Bible Text: Matthew 14:22-33
Story Focus: Peter's initial faith in Jesus faltered when he attempted to walk on the water to meet Jesus. After Jesus rescued him, Peter and the disciples believed that Jesus was God's son.
Faith Focus: When we focus on Jesus, we can do more than we think we can.

Anticipated Outcomes

1. The children will learn that although Peter trusted in Jesus, he still got into trouble and depended upon Jesus to help him out. Jesus accepted Peter even when he faltered.

2. The children will realize that Jesus loves them and accepts them all the time, even when they feel they have failed him. Jesus will help them do what they do not think is possible in relationships and in their daily living.

Materials

- A large, simple wooden cross
- A cloth "mast" of a ship draped over the cross
- Other props as desired: a boat with oars
- Chorus for the weather, or appropriate sound effects on a tape recorder
- Costumes for Peter, Jesus, and disciples (same as Session 1)

Worship

Sing songs (see pages 51-60). Pray.

Introduction

The drama can be introduced by one of the characters or by the Worship leader. While the introduction is being given, the characters put on their costumes and get into the boat so they are ready with the rhyme to begin the drama.

Leader: Yesterday in our drama we met Simon and Andrew. They were fishing when Jesus came up to them and invited them to become "fishers of people" and follow Jesus. At the end of their first meeting, Jesus gave Simon a new name. The name "Peter" meant "rock" in the Greek language. Jesus was telling Peter that he was going to be a strong, faithful follower of his. And Peter was. But sometimes even strong people run into trouble when they don't give their full attention to Jesus. Watch and listen to the story to find out what happened to Peter today.

Present the Bible story drama, "Peter Walks on Water–Not!"

Dismissal

After the drama, dismiss the children to their various activities. Make sure that the Group leaders know the order of the rotation.

PETER WALKS ON THE WATER–NOT!

Cast: Peter, Jesus, three disciples, chorus for the weather (involve the junior youth group)

Setting: *The open sea. The net has been removed from the cross and is replaced by the mast of a fishing boat. Peter and the disciples are in the boat rowing. Sing the first two All parts to the tune of "Row, Row, Row Your Boat."*

All: Row, row, row your boat
       Down on Galilee.
       It's just luck we're still afloat
       A fisherman's life for me!

Disciple 1: What a day!

Disciple 2: You can say that again.

Disciple 1: Okay. What a day!

Disciple 3: It was a day. Definitely.

[*Wind sounds from chorus.*]

Peter: Save your wind for rowing. There's a bad storm coming up.

All: Row, row with all your might;
       The wind is getting bad.
       Simon Peter's all uptight;
       Mustn't make him mad.

Disciple 1: All those people were waiting when we arrived with Jesus.

Disciple 3: Waiting! Definitely waiting.

Disciple 2: I didn't realize what was happening at first. They were sitting down after Jesus finished teaching, and we were going around handing out the food, and it just kept coming!

Disciple 1: Yes! I kept thinking, this has to be the last piece. But when I stuck my hand back in my basket, there was more. Out of nowhere!

Disciple 3: Definitely nowhere!

Disciple 1: And it all came from that small boy's lunch. Was it three loaves and six fish? No . . . two loaves and five fish?

Disciple 2: No. It was five loaves and two fish.

Disciple 3: Five loaves and two fish, definitely.

Disciple 1: How did Jesus do it? It was like, I mean, Wow!

Disciple 3: Like wow. Definitely like wow.

Peter: Cut the talking and row! We're beginning to take in water.

Disciple 3: Row, row, r . . .

All: Shut up!

Disciple 2: Where is Jesus now?

Disciple 1: When it got dark he stayed behind to send all the people home. Then he was going up the mountainside to be alone and to pray.

Peter: He said he would meet us on the other side, but . . . [*Rowing hard*] with . . . this wind . . . [*Pause*], I said: "WITH THIS WIND" [*Chorus makes wind noises quickly*]. Thank you. With . . . this . . . wind . . . I don't know . . . if we'll ever . . . get there.

Disciple 2: They wanted to make Jesus king. It would be nice to have a king for a friend.

Disciple 3: Yes! . . . [*All look expectantly at him*] . . . definitely?

[*All resume rowing. Disciple 3 looks at audience and shrugs. Jesus enters.*]

Disciple 1: What is THAT? [*Points ahead*].

Disciple 2: It looks like someone walking towards the boat.

Peter: But we're in the middle of the lake!

Disciple 1: Well, look for yourself. I think it's a ghost.

Disciple 3: Definitely a ghost. Engage reverse thrusters!

[*All row in reverse frantically except for Peter who clambers over them to the prow of the boat to cries of "Watch it," "Ow, my foot," "You clumsy ox," "Didn't your father teach you never to stand up in a boat?"*]

Peter: Wait! It looks like Jesus. It's so dark, I can hardly see. [*Calls*] Is that you, Lord?

Jesus: Yes, it is I. Do not be afraid.

Peter: If it is really you, Lord, let me come to you.

Jesus: Well, then come.

[*Peter looks at the disciples, swings one leg over the side, tests the water gingerly with a foot. Shows surprise and delight. Swings other leg over and tries a few steps while holding onto the boat. As he gains confidence, he begins walking towards Jesus. Chorus huddles, then tiptoes up behind Peter.*]

Chorus: 1, 2, 3, BOOM!

Peter: Help me, Lord!

Jesus: Come to me. Don't mind the storm.

Chorus: BOOOOOOM! [*Peter is on his stomach.*]

Jesus: Come on, you can do better than that. Give me your hand.

[*Peter swim-crawls to Jesus who helps him up. They return to the boat hand in hand, Peter following behind with his eyes tightly shut. Meanwhile Chorus has linked arms and is humming the tune of "The Blue Danube."*]

Chorus: Boom, boom, boom, boom, boom, whoosh-whoosh, whoosh-whoosh

[*This is repeated as Jesus and Peter enter the boat. Jesus eyes the Chorus sternly with hands on hips. Chorus tiptoes away quietly.*]

All: [*Kneeling*] You must be the son of God. Are you the Messiah? Are you the one we have been waiting for?

Jesus: Wait! I will teach you all these things, but let's get to shore first. We've all had a long day.

Disciple 3: Yes. A long day. Definitely.

[*Exit rowing.*]

Permission is granted to photocopy pages 38 and 39 for drama presenters.

Session 3

An Invitation to Loyalty

Theme: From Loyalty to Betrayal
Bible Texts: John 13:34-38, Mark 14:66-72
Biblical Background: John 13:1-38; John 18:1-11; Luke 22:51; John 19:1–20:1-23
Story Focus: Peter wanted to be a loyal friend to Jesus, but when frightening things that he did not understand began to happen, he denied the friendship. Even though Peter did not pass the loyalty test, Jesus continued to love him.
Faith Focus: It is easy to slip back into old patterns of behaviour when we are faced with new and frightening situations. Jesus continues to love and forgive us even when we do not act like his friend.

Anticipated Outcomes

1. The children will learn that although Peter disappointed Jesus and himself, Jesus still loved him and was willing to forgive him.

2. The children will recognize that there is forgiveness for them when they disappoint themselves and/or their friends.

Materials

- A large simple wooden cross with no symbol on it
- Props for the mime scenes (sword, helmets, serving tray, shawls)

Worship

Sing songs (see pages 51-60). Pray.

Introduction

The drama can be introduced by one of the characters or by the Worship leader. Characters put on their costumes and prepare for the drama. This drama can be done as a simple monologue by Peter. Scenes to mime have been suggested at various places in the monologue. If the miming is done, make sure that it does not detract from the words that Peter is saying and from the somber atmosphere intended.

Leader: Yesterday our friend Simon Peter learned about having faith or trusting in Jesus to do the impossible. He believed that he could walk on the water, but lost his faith when he realized what was happening. Sometimes Peter acted without thinking things through, especially when he became excited. But Jesus reached out his hand and rescued Peter. Together they walked on the water. Jesus was a pretty good friend for Peter, wasn't he? He didn't yell at him for not trusting in him. Jesus just held out his hand and helped his friend. He knew that friends are there for you, to help you in tough times.

Peter was trying to be a good friend to Jesus, too. But sometimes he messed up. Then Peter did not feel very good about himself. Listen to Peter tell about one time when he was not very proud of himself as a friend.

Present the Bible drama, "What Are Friends For?"

Dismissal

After the drama, dismiss the children to their various activities. Make sure that the Group leaders know the order of the rotation.

WHAT ARE FRIENDS FOR?

Cast: Peter, Others (three or four people)

Note: Peter gives the narration as a monologue. On several occasions he steps "into" the mime scenes and reenacts the scene as he speaks. The other characters "come to life" but mime actors do not speak. In order to maintain the solemn nature of the story, the other characters must not detract from Peter's words. Miming instructions are given at the appropriate places.

As an alternative to the mimed scenes, Peter can tell the story dramatically.

Setting: *Shoreline. The cross is empty and the room is darkened.*

Peter: I suppose you are wondering why I am all alone walking along a windy beach in the dark of a cold spring morning. I must tell you about the darkest, saddest day of my whole life. We had been following Jesus for about three years, and we thought that we knew him pretty well. We could tell that this morning Jesus had something serious on his mind.

[*At one side of the stage, Jesus and two disciples are in silent conversation. Peter enters the scene and continues his monologue. The other characters mime what Peter is saying.*]

We had made preparations to celebrate the Jewish Passover feast in the upstairs room of a friend's house in Jerusalem. We did not know that this would be the last meal that we would have with Jesus before he died. We were busy with our own ideas about what his teaching meant for us. We all felt we were important to Jesus' plans. You can imagine how shocked we were when Jesus suddenly said, "One of you is going to betray me." We all started saying, "Is it I, Lord?" "Surely you can't mean me." "Who could it possibly be?"

I was angry that one of us who had been Jesus' trusted friend for so long would do something like that. So I said, "Lord, even if everyone else deserts you, you can count on me!" And I meant it.

Jesus looked straight into my eyes and said, "Listen to me, Peter. Before you hear the rooster crowing again, you will have denied that you even know me."

That nearly broke my heart! After all that I had left behind for him, after all that we had been through together, how could he think so little of me?

[*Pause, while mime group assumes "frozen positions."*]

After the meal we all went to the park where Jesus sometimes went to pray. I'm ashamed to say I don't know how long we were there, because we were all too tired to think about Jesus' problems. We fell asleep. After he had prayed for a while, he came and woke us up and warned us that soldiers were coming for him. [*Pause.*]

[*Two of the characters become soldiers who stand on either side of Jesus. Peter enters the scene, acting as he speaks.*]

This was my chance to show him that I would stick by him no matter what! I jumped between Jesus and the soldiers. I whipped out my sword and slashed at the head of the nearest soldier. Down he went, but he was still alive. I had sliced only his ear. I raised my sword to finish the job . . . but suddenly Jesus was standing in the way. "Put away your sword, Peter," he said. Then he touched the soldier and healed his ear.

[*Pause, while mime group freezes in position.*]

You may think I was very brave. Perhaps I was. I only know that at the time I did not really think. I just acted. I mean, there were the temple police, with the backing of the whole Roman army. It just didn't matter any more. I knew I would probably get killed. Why not kill some of the soldiers before I got killed!

But Jesus stopped me. Suddenly it was out of my hands. I didn't know what he wanted from me. I felt I was the one being betrayed, not being allowed to do what I knew I could. It all seemed hopeless. I dropped my sword and ran, following the other disciples who had fled into the night.

Soon I stopped running. I wanted to know what was happening to my best friend, so I followed the crowd to the temple court where they were holding Jesus.

I am so ashamed about what happened next.

[*Peter steps into the action. Jesus is not present. The other two become servants in the courtyard.*]

As I stood in the courtyard warming my hands over a campfire, a slave girl thought she recognized me as one of Jesus' friends. I said I didn't know what she was talking about–that I had never even heard of a man named Jesus. Then the rooster crowed.

[*Sound of a rooster, characters freeze, then pause in silence for about forty-five seconds.*]

To this very day, there is no worse sound in all the world than a rooster crowing. But even now, if I could have my way, with my strength and with my sword, I would gladly fight for him until I am killed. That's how I do things. But his talk of the meek inheriting the earth and not striking back and turning the other cheek when someone slaps you . . . I don't know how to do that! His way is so different! He seems to have so much love for everyone. I felt so worthless. That was why I ran away. I feel so afraid and helpless. It is as though we are playing a new game, and no one has told us the rules.

So here I am, trying to sort things out on a dark, windy beach, waiting for the sun to rise. Will it ever get light again? There's one more thing, one terrible, wonderful thing: some of the women in our group have been to the grave where they laid Jesus' body after he died, and they are saying that his body is gone. They say an angel told them that he is alive again, that we will see him soon. Can it be true? Is he alive? How will I ever be able to face him again? Do you think my best friend will forgive me?

I can't stand this any longer. I'm going to find out for myself. Can he really be alive? There's just one thing I do feel certain about: it cannot all end here, with footprints on an empty beach.

[*Peter exits.*]

Permission is granted to photocopy pages 41 and 42 for drama presenters.

Session 4

An Invitation to Courage

Theme: From Fear to Courage
Bible Text: Acts 2:1-42
Story Focus: At Pentecost, God's Spirit changed Peter from a fearful follower to a courageous leader. Peter was no longer afraid to tell others about Jesus when he realized that the Holy Spirit was helping him.
Faith Focus: When we let God's Holy Spirit live in us, we are given courage to act boldly for Jesus.

Anticipated Outcomes

1. The children will learn about the role of the Holy Spirit in helping the disciples to carry out Jesus' ministry after he left them.

2. The children will be introduced to the person of the Holy Spirit as one who helps them follow Jesus.

Materials

- Cross
- Headbands made from orange and yellow crepe or tissue paper twisted together that either sit on the head or can be tied around the forehead (minimum 5)
- Costume for the Holy Spirit in fire colours (orange and yellow)

The Holy Spirit should look mysterious and "other-worldly" but not like a space alien or ghost. Peter can see the Holy Spirit but the other disciples cannot.

Worship

Sing songs (see pages 51-60). Pray.

Introduction

The drama can be introduced by one of the drama troupe or by the Worship leader. Characters put on their costumes and prepare for the drama.

Leader: Yesterday we learned that Simon Peter was not as good a friend as he thought he would be. Remember how he promised to stick with Jesus no matter what, and how he even used his sword to defend his best friend, Jesus? When Jesus told him that fighting was not the way to demonstrate loyalty, Peter ran away and left Jesus alone. Then he lied about his friendship with Jesus. He told the servant girl that he didn't know anything about that man Jesus. Then he heard that sound–the rooster crowing! He went away and cried because he had betrayed his friend just as Jesus had predicted he would.

Deep inside himself, Peter knew that Jesus still loved him. When he heard that Jesus died on the cross, he became very sad. He hoped that Jesus would forgive him and they could be friends again. Jesus did forgive him! They had a happy meeting on the seashore one day. Jesus asked Peter to be the leader of the group when he went away to heaven. Peter knew then that Jesus still considered him "The Rock" and trusted him to be a good leader.

Today's story takes place in a house where all of Jesus' disciples have gathered to plan for a future without Jesus as their leader. They are all sad, worried, and frightened about what will happen to their little group. Something happened that changed everything for them. Watch and see how the disciples were changed dramatically.

Present the Bible drama, "Changed!"

Dismissal

After the drama, dismiss the children to their various activities.

CHANGED!

Cast: Peter, Holy Spirit, three disciples

Setting: *A room. The headbands hang on the cross. The Holy Spirit will take them off the cross and place the bands on the heads of the disciples during the drama.*

Disciple 1: All of Jesus' friends found out one way or another that he was alive. Many of us saw him with our very own eyes. And some of us were there when he went to heaven.

Disciple 2: We are no longer brokenhearted that he died, but we do not know what to expect next . . . except trouble! We are known as the friends of a condemned criminal, and we could be arrested and treated like Jesus was at any time.

Disciple 3: But even if there is danger, we better get organized. We have to figure out where we are going to live, to whom it is safe to speak about Jesus, how we can feed ourselves, and all kinds of other problems.

Peter: Everyone is always asking me everything, as though I would know all the answers.

Disciple 1: Peter, where do these sandals go?

Peter: I don't know.

Disciple 2: Peter, what's for supper tonight?

Peter: I don't know.

Disciple 3: Peter, will the Roman army catch us and torture us?

Peter: I don't know.

Disciple 1: Peter, where's my drinking cup?

Peter: I don't know.

Disciple 2: Peter, why is a circle round?

Peter: I don't know.

Disciple 3: Peter, is someone who is twenty-five just old, real old, or very, very old?

Peter: I DON'T KNOW!!

All: Don't you know ANYTHING?

Peter: [*Whimpering*] I don't know.

Holy Spirit: [*Speaks while taking the headbands from the cross and placing them on his arm.*] When the day of Pentecost had come, they were all together in one place. Suddenly a sound came from heaven like a rush of mighty wind, and it filled all the house where they were sitting. There appeared to them tongues, as of fire, resting on each of them. They were all filled with the Holy Spirit and began to speak in other tongues, as the Spirit gave them ability.

[*During this time the Holy Spirit enters, removes the headbands from the cross and moves around the group. Beginning softly and growing louder are wind sounds made by the group. Peter looks puzzled at first, then increasingly alarmed. The flames are the bands that the Holy Spirit has taken from the cross and now places on the heads of the disciples. Tongues can be symbolized by greetings in Spanish, German, and other languages. This scene is to be upbeat and joyful. The Holy Spirit moves slowly centre backstage and watches with folded arms.*]

Disciple 3: WOW! What was that?

Peter: That must have been the Holy Spirit that Jesus told us to wait for.

Disciple 2: What were those words I was saying?

Peter: You were speaking a rare dialect from the coastal town of Pontus.

Disciple 1: I still haven't found my . . .

Peter: Your drinking cup is on the window ledge.

All: Peter, you finally have some answers.

Peter: [*Pleased with himself*] Yeah, I kinda do, don't I?

[*Disciples 1, 2, and 3 remove headbands and become the crowd (put on other hats) sitting to one side. The Holy Spirit comes behind Peter, nodding toward the crowd. Peter looks terrified. The Holy Spirit taps, nudges, prods, and finally shoves Peter toward the crowd. Peter swallows, looks around at the Holy Spirit pleadingly, gets a thumbs-up signal, and begins to speak, tentatively at first, but then with growing confidence.*]

Peter: Well . . . uh . . . [*Coughs*] I uh . . . [*Crowd gets fidgety, but settles down again*] I suppose . . . uh . . . you all think we're acting kind of crazy here. But we're not high, or drunk, or anything like that. This is what the prophets said would happen . . . uh . . . [*To Holy Spirit*] where was that?

Holy Spirit: In the Book of Joel.

Peter: In the Book of Joel: I will pour out my Spirit on all people. Your sons and daughters shall prophesy . . . your cousins shall. . . .

Holy Spirit: Young men, YOUNG MEN!

Peter: Sorry. Young men shall see visions. Okay so far?

Holy Spirit: You're doing great!

Peter: Thanks.

Disciple 2: To whom is he speaking?

Disciple 1: I don't see anyone.

Disciple 3: But someone is helping him, definitely.

Peter: Now listen to me! You all heard about Jesus of Nazareth. In spite of all he taught you and in spite of all the miracles you saw him do, you killed him. God raised him from death, and we all saw him alive. All of you should know that Jesus is the Messiah we've all been waiting for, and that he rules from heaven right now.

[*There is silence, then the crowd whispers among themselves. Peter looks back nervously at the Holy Spirit who shrugs patiently. The crowd gets to its feet as each speaks.*]

Disciple 1: But we didn't know.

Disciple 2: It looks as if we made a big mistake.

Disciple 3: We wish someone had told us.

All: What can we do?

[*Peter and the Holy Spirit share a thumbs-up.*]

Peter: If you are really sorry, and believe that Jesus is the Messiah, just admit to God you were wrong. Be baptized, and you too will receive the Holy Spirit. Do you want to do that?

All: Yes!

Peter: All three . . . thousand of you?

All: YES!

Peter and Holy Spirit: Yessssss! [*Give high five symbol and walk off arm in arm.*]

Peter: All right then–follow me.

[*Peter and Holy Spirit chat to each other as they move toward exit.*]

Holy Spirit: Well, that worked out okay.

Peter: Yes, I was worried there for a moment. Do you think I should be speaking louder?

Holy Spirit: No, but perhaps you can brush up on your sense of timing.

Disciple 1: I still can't see with whom he is talking. Look how he's holding his arm out in the fresh air. [*Follows after Peter, mimicking him.*]

Disciple 2: But Peter certainly has changed! [*Exits with a puzzled look.*]

Disciple 3: Changed? Definitely! [*Shrugs and follows after the others.*]

Session 5

An Invitation to Acceptance

Theme: From Rejection to Acceptance
Bible Text: Acts 10:1-48
Story Focus: After a vision from God, Peter believed that it was not right for him to be prejudiced against people who were not Jews. All people are equally accepted by God.
Faith Focus: When we think like God, we value all people as God does.

Anticipated Outcomes

1. The children will learn that Peter became a changed person when he was able to accept people who were not Jews as equal followers of Jesus.

2. The children will recognize that God wants them to treat everyone with respect, even the people who are very different.

Materials

- Cross
- A plain bedsheet or tablecloth
- Stuffed animals that would have been "unclean" to Jews
- Headbands from Session 4
- Soldier helmet for Cornelius

Worship

Sing songs (see pages 51-60). Pray.

Introduction

The drama can be introduced by one of the drama troupe or by the Worship leader. Characters put on their costumes and prepare for the drama.

Leader: In yesterday's drama, we found out how Simon Peter changed from a hesitant, cautious disciple to a bold preacher and leader. Finally, he was showing those "rock-like" characteristics that Jesus saw in him on the seashore when he was a fisherman. But God was not finished with Peter yet. Peter had more changing to do in his attitudes toward other people.

Present the Bible drama, "Everyone Belongs."

Dismissal

After the drama, dismiss the children to their various activities.

EVERYONE BELONGS

Cast: The Holy Spirit, Peter, Cornelius, two servants

Setting: *A house by the sea. The arms of the cross support a bulging sheet fitted with strings on the corners that can be lowered. Find a creative person to design this set. In the sheet are stuffed animals, rubber snakes, etc.*

Holy Spirit: In the town of Caesarea there was a Roman officer.

[*Cornelius, left front posing "soldierly," gives alms to imaginary beggar, etc.*]

He was a good man who, with his whole family, loved God very much. He gave to charities and prayed regularly. [*Cornelius kneels.*]

One day a messenger from God spoke to him.

[*Holy Spirit taps Cornelius on the back of the head. He falls forward.*]

Cornelius, God has heard your prayers. Now send for Peter. He is in Joppa at Simon the tanner's house. [*Cornelius joins Others backstage left.*]

Meanwhile, in a house by the seashore, Peter was praying. [*Peter kneels at right.*]

Suddenly he fell into a trance. [*Holy Spirit taps Peter.*]

I love my work. Now watch.

[*Holy Spirit lets down the sheet. Peter peers inside.*]

Peter: Eeeyuch! Snakes! And spiders! And . . . liver! Pheeooow!

Holy Spirit: Take and eat.

Peter: Uh-uh! [*Shakes head*] It is forbidden for a Jew to eat some of that stuff. And broccoli should be on the list. No way!

Holy Spirit: Way! If God has cleansed a thing, you should never treat it as unclean again. [*To audience with exasperation*] This had to be repeated three times, and he still didn't get it [*Holy Spirit dips sheet twice and hoists it up again*]. Then the sheet was lifted back into heaven.

[*Cornelius and Others who are his servants approach Peter. Cornelius points to Peter.*]

Now Listen, Peter, some Romans are coming. You will go with them, and no more questions.

Peter: [*Shrugs*] You're the boss.

Holy Spirit: At least we got that right.

Servant 1: [*To Peter*] Please, sir. Our master would like you to come back with us.

Peter: Weeell. I don't know. . . .

Servant 2: Pleease! [*Holy Spirit pushes Peter forward.*]

Peter: Okay. Okay! I'm going. There is no need to shove me.

Servant 1: [*Whispering behind hand*] What's going on here? Did you push him?

Servant 2: Never touched him. He acts as though he is speaking to someone else.

Servant 1: Weird, definitely. Will you follow us? Please, sir?

[*All move to Cornelius.*]

Peter: As you know, we Jews think that you Romans are unclean people, and we are not to go even into your homes. But God is teaching us something new. So when your servants came, I followed them without hesitation.

Holy Spirit: Ha!

[*Peter shushes him, finger to lips. Holy Spirit mimics him.*]

Cornelius: Four days ago while I was praying, a person in bright clothing appeared to me [*Peter looks questioning at the Holy Spirit who nods vigorously and points to self*] and who told me to send for you. I have brought together all these people to hear what God has told you.

Peter: I can see now that God accepts everyone who loves God and wants to be obedient to God. Well, let me tell you about Jesus. We saw how God anointed him when John baptized him. And we were there when Jesus healed the sick and did other miracles. [*Peter, lost in his own eloquence, wanders to front of stage.*]

Then–this part will knock your sandals off–Jesus died a criminal's death on the cross, but God brought him back to life!

[*Holy Spirit sneaks behind the Others and places headbands on their heads. They look at each other with amazement and begin to speak in other languages.*]

All: Preist den Herrn! Praise the Lord! Alabare a mi Senor! Alleluia! Louez a Dieu! [*One voice in southern accent: Well, Ah'm jest gonna lee-if' mah hayan's an' pea-raze ya, La-ord!*] What language is THAT!!??

Peter: Puleeze! I'm not finished yet. That bit comes later.

Holy Spirit: Lighten up, Peter. You can't decide when I am to touch people's lives. Or do you think they are faking it?

Peter: Well, no. It looks like the real thing to me.

Holy Spirit: What real thing?

Peter: The thing that happened to us.

Holy Spirit: Sooo?

Peter: So . . . Don't rush me . . . It's coming. . . . So God zapped the wrong ones? [*Holy Spirit shakes head.*] They're really Jews who were kidnapped as babies and . . . no? . . . I know! God loves everybody in the same way, no matter who they are or how they look or what colour their eyes are. Or what flavour ice cream they like or where they live or. . . .

Holy Spirit: Enough already! When he gets it, by George, he gets it.

Peter: You all believe in God exactly as I do! There's nothing to stop me from baptizing you right now. Who is ready?

All: Me! Me! Me! [*Crowd around Peter chatter excitedly and exit.*]

Permission is granted to photocopy pages 48 and 49 for drama presenters.

Songs

Hallelujah Ballad—Peter

Text: Joy MacKenzie
Music: John E. Coates
Descant: Susan Pries

51 WORSHIP RESOURCE

One in Love

ONE	IN	LOVE

Right hand	*Right fingertips move into left finger circle*	*Arms crossed on chest (hands in fists)*

ONE	IN	FRIENDSHIP	TRUE
"	"	*Hook index fingers: 1st move: rt. finger over lf. 2nd move: lf. finger over right.*	*Rt. index finger on mouth and move straight out two times.*

ONE	IN	HOPE
"	"	*Cross index and 3rd fingers of each hand (like for 'good luck') and "jump" hands slightly forward.*

ONE IN SPIRIT

TOO

Index finger on both hands bump together pointing straight out in front.

Rt. and lf. separate in wavy motion (like pulling a thread).

ONE	IN	FAITH
"	"	*(Rt. and lf. thumb holds index finger down; other fingers straight.) Rt. vertical hand on top of lf. vertical hand.*

THAT

GOD

 Lf. palm arcs down from above head to forehead.

WILL

CARE

 Rt. and lf. both form "v" and side-by-side circle horizon: tally (left to right).

FOR

 Rt. index on fore-head twists outward.

YOU

Rt. index points to other person.

TILL

WE

 *Rt. hand (forms "W") on right side of chest; circles to left side.*

MEET

 *Both hands form #1 and move together to meet in front of chest.*

TOGETHER

 *Fists together circle horizontally right to left (fists with thumb between index and 3rd finger).*

AGAIN

Lf. palm vertical. Rt. fingertips, bent a bit, move left to touch heel of lf. palm.

One in Love

One in love, one in friend-ship true. __ one in hope, one in spir - it, too. __ one in faith that God will care for you __ till we meet to - ge - ther a - gain. __

Words and music: Judith A. Helms
Copyright © 1989 Judith A. Helms. Used by permission.

Fisherman Peter

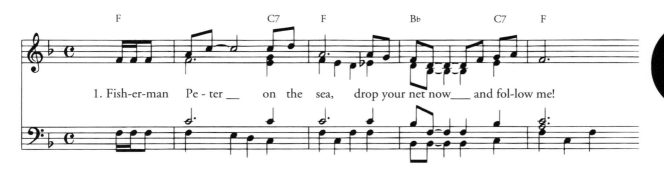

1. Fish-er-man Pe - ter __ on the sea, drop your net now___ and fol-low me!

Fish-er-man Pe - ter __ on the sea, drop your net now____ and fol-low me!

2. Fisherman James on the sea . . .
3. Fisherman John on the sea . . .
4. Fisherman *(insert child's name)* on the sea . . .

Words and music: South Carolina spiritual

Discipleship

broth - er, see that he is fed.
prais - es in both words and song.
peo - ple how the world should be.

I can show my sis - ter kind - ness and care.
I'll be friends with oth - ers who aren't like me.
Fam - 'ly, friends, and neigh - bors, en - e - mies, too:

I can show my friends that I know how to share.
They be - long to Je - sus: we all do, you see.
Get a - long to - geth - er— that's what we can do.

The Lord Is My Shepherd

Group 1: The Lord is my shep - herd, I'll walk with him al - ways.

Group 2: He knows me and he loves me, I'll walk with him al - ways.
He gave his life to save me, I'll walk with him al - ways.
He's liv - ing now and helps me, I'll walk with him al - ways.
He cares for me and guides me. I'll walk with him al - ways.
He says, "Fear not. I'm with you." I'll walk with him al - ways.

Chorus: Groups 1 and 2

Al - ways, al - ways, I'll walk with him al - ways.

Based on Psalm 23
Traditional

Child of God

1. If an-y-bod-y asks you who I am, who I am,
2. If an-y-bod-y asks you who we are, who we are,

who I am; If an-y-bod-y asks you who I am,
who we are; If an-y-bod-y asks you who we are,

tell them I'm a child___ of God.
tell them we're the fam-ily of God.

Southern Folk Song

Jesus Cares for His People

(Tune: Let Us Break Bread Together)

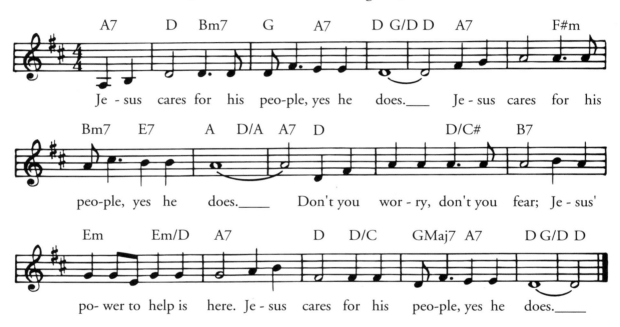

Je - sus cares for his peo-ple, yes he does.___ Je - sus cares for his

peo-ple, yes he does.___ Don't you wor - ry, don't you fear; Je - sus'

po- wer to help is here. Je - sus cares for his peo-ple, yes he does.___

Text: Anne Neufeld Rupp
Music: American folk hymn

Then and Now Resource

Then and Now Resource

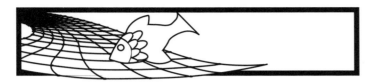

Introduction

Programme

Then and Now is the part of the programme in which the children learn the memory text, retell or review the Bible story, and talk about the meaning of the story. Each Then and Now time includes three activities: Bible memory, Bible story reinforcement, and Application. As the leader, you will have to schedule time for each of these three activities within the time allotted. Spend about seven minutes on the memory work each day. The story retelling and application activities are both important. In reviewing the Bible story, children are committing God's good news to their memory. In story application, children reflect on the meaning of God's story in their personal lives.

Leadership

See Leaders and responsibilities, page 13. The leader should have good communication skills with children, enjoy memory work, have an interest in drama, and be able to stimulate discussion. Many of the suggestions for retelling the Bible story and the application work best with small groups of children. Expect the active participation of the Group leaders who come with the children. Group leaders can help small groups with the art and creative dramas. Let these leaders know what you expect of them. Write out instructions for each day and ask them to come prepared to help. Encourage them to continue and/or build on the discussions with their own group at the end of the day.

Preparation

Read through the entire Then and Now Resource to have a complete understanding of this part of the programme. Prepare the memory work materials ahead of time and begin the review as soon as the children arrive.

Collect clothing from members of the congregation and/or thrift shops. Have enough dress-up clothing so that each person will have something to put on. Have all supplies on hand before the session begins.

Bible memory

2 Peter 1:3, 5-7 has been chosen for two reasons. Simon Peter probably wrote

Memory Text

2 Peter 1:3, 5-7 (NRSV)

[3][God's] divine power has given us everything needed for life and godliness, through the knowledge of him who called us by his own glory and goodness.

[5]For this very reason, you must make every effort to support your faith with goodness, and goodness with knowledge, [6]and knowledge with self-control, and self-control with endurance, and endurance with godliness, [7]and godliness with mutual affection, and mutual affection with love.

Memory Text

2 Peter 1:3, 5-7 (NIV)

[3]His divine power has given us everything we need for life and godliness through our knowledge of him who called us by his own glory and goodness.

[5]For this very reason, make every effort to add to your faith goodness; and to goodness, knowledge; [6]and to knowledge, self-control; and to self-control, perseverance; and to perseverance, godliness; [7]and to godliness, brotherly kindness; and to brotherly kindness, love.

these words. This passage states the central theme of the curriculum, that everyone can be changed by the power of God. See pages 63-64 for the Bible text.

Use a variety of methods to help the children learn this text. A quick, concentrated review daily will help them learn the text during the week. Make copies (pages 63 or 64) for the children to decorate and take home as a reminder of their adventure with Simon Peter.

Bible Memory Review

2 _____ 1:3, 5-7 (NRSV)

• •

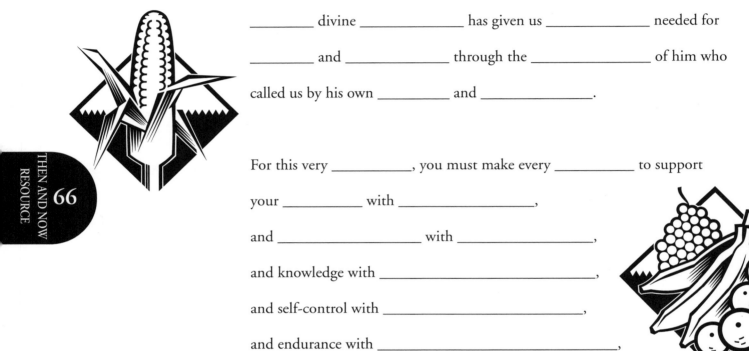

_____ divine _____ has given us _____ needed for _____ and _____ through the _____ of him who called us by his own _____ and _____.

For this very _____, you must make every _____ to support your _____ with _____,

and _____ with _____,

and knowledge with _____,

and self-control with _____,

and endurance with _____,

and godliness with _____ _____,

and mutual affection with _____.

• •

mutual affection	knowledge	love	everything
godliness	life	glory	power
self-control	endurance	goodness	Peter
His	goodness	godliness	God's
reason	effort	knowledge	faith

Permission is granted to photocopy this page.

Picture Bible Memory (Good News Bible)

Picture Bible Memory (Good News Bible)

ANSWERS

2 (Peter) ter 1:3

G's (God's) (divine) (power) has

(given) us (everything) we (need)

2 (to) (live) a (truly) (religious) (life)

(through) (our) (knowledge) of the 1 (one)

(who) (called) us 2 (to) (share) in G's (God's)

own (glory) (and) (goodness).

Session plans

Session 1

An Invitation to Follow

> **Theme**: From Fisherman to Follower
> **Bible Text**: Mark 1:16-20; Luke 5:1-11
> **Biblical Background**: Mark 1:1-31
> **Story Focus**: Peter was a fisherman who chose to give up his nets and his job to become a follower of Jesus. This was the beginning of a relationship with Jesus that would change his entire life.
> **Faith Focus**: Jesus invites us to become his followers for life.

Anticipated Outcomes

1. The children will memorize 2 Peter 1:3.
2. The children will re-enact the Bible story. (See Worship, pp. 31-60.)
3. The children will understand, at an age-appropriate level, what it means to be invited to follow Jesus.

Materials

- Memory verse printed on chart paper or chalkboard (See pages 63-64.)
- Cutout pieces of construction paper to cover key words
- Box(es) with costumes, towels, head ties, fishing props
- Paper, markers, string, and clothespins for a time line
- Names of occupations written or drawn on slips of paper

Method

Bible memory

1. Display the memory verse and read it several times together.
2. Cover or erase several key words (*God's, power, knowledge*) and continue to repeat the verse aloud.
3. Continue to cover or erase words as the group repeats the verse until only the small words remain.

Bible story reinforcement

1. Invite the group to give the chronological order of the Bible story. Write the key actions on paper or the chalkboard. If using paper, have two children hold up a string line and attach the papers with the action words to the string with clothespins or fasten the string to the wall.

2. Divide the children into groups of five or six. Have them choose something from the costume box and pick a character from the story. Extra characters can be people who work in the fishing business, or children on the shore. One person from the group can narrate the story, using the time line as a guide, while the others act out the story.

Application

1. Distribute slips of paper with the names or pictures of occupations, one per child.

2. Get into groups, each with one adult. The adult, playing the role of Jesus, will invite each child, in turn, to demonstrate (mime) her or his occupation. Then "Jesus" extends a hand, saying, "_____(child's name), come, be my friend and follower." Continue until everyone is part of the circle.

3. With hands joined, invite responses from the children on how they can follow Jesus ("To me, following Jesus means ...").

4. Close with a prayer, thanking Jesus for inviting us to be his friend.

5. Dismiss the group to the next activity.

Additional ideas

Instead of having children act out occupations, talk about ways that people show they are following Jesus. How can the children follow Jesus wherever they are?

Session 2

An Invitation to Faith

Theme: From Faith to Failure to Faith
Bible Text: Matthew 14:22-33
Story Focus: Peter's initial faith in Jesus faltered when he attempted to walk on the water to meet Jesus. After Jesus rescued him, Peter and the disciples believed that Jesus was God's special son.
Faith Focus: When we focus on Jesus, we can do more than we think we can.

Anticipated Outcomes

1. The children will complete memorization of 2 Peter 1:3.

2. The children will retell the Bible story by drawing pictures for an accordion book.

3. The children will reflect on personal difficulties that require trust in God.

Materials

- Bible verse from Session 1
- Picture Bible Memory, page 67, with pictures or symbols for the key Scripture words (Adapt to fit the Bible translation you are using.)
- Pens, markers, crayons, or chalk
- Slips of paper with captions for the Bible story
- Accordion books for each child made from three pieces of standard white paper or construction paper (See illustration.)

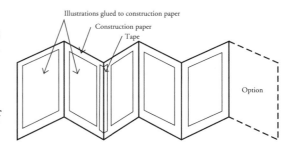

Illustrations glued to construction paper
Construction paper
Tape
Option

Method

Bible memory

1. Display the memory verse (see page 63 or 64) and read it several times together.

2. Cover all the words that can be replaced by the symbols. You may wish to enlarge these pictures in order to cover the words. You could also make several copies (one per group) and glue them to light cardboard. Cover both sides with adhesive-backed clear plastic. Use sticky tack or masking tape to attach to the bristol board or the chalkboard. Store the pieces in plastic ziplock bags and encourage the children to put the pictures in order during Gather and Greet or Gather and Bless.

3. Repeat the verse together several times.

Bible story reinforcement

1. Review the story by listing the key actions in the order that they happened. For younger children, have simple captions prepared on slips of paper that can be glued onto each page of the accordion book. Older children can print their own captions.

The accordion book should have enough space for a cover picture and four pictures with captions. Captions for the younger children could be:
- Peter Walks on Water! (title page)
- A Stormy Night at Sea
- Jesus Walks Toward the Boat
- Peter Walks on Water–NOT!
- Jesus Saves Peter
- The Disciples Worship Jesus (end page)

2. Distribute prefolded and taped accordion booklets, captions, and markers to each child. Instruct the children to draw simple pictures to illustrate each caption.

3. When they have finished, invite each child to find a partner and tell each other the story.

Application

1. Form into groups that each have an adult. Invite the children to think of something that is difficult for them to do. Encourage honesty and respect for each other. On chart paper, make a list of things that are difficult for children to do.

2. Make another list of things that can help us overcome our difficulties.

3. Remind the children that God listens to us and wants to help us when we have difficulties. Invite the children to sit silently and talk to Jesus about the difficult things they have to do.

4. Close with a prayer, thanking God for listening to our prayers and for promising to be with us when we are happy and when things are tough for us.

5. Dismiss the children to their next activity.

Additional ideas

Creative Drama (for older children)

If the children and resource leader enjoy creative drama, try retelling the story using "tableau" scenes instead of drawing. Each tableau focuses on a different emotion that would be experienced by the characters.

Invite children to form into groups of five to eight people. Each group is one "fishing crew" made up of Peter and several disciples. The resource leader will call out instructions, when to freeze, and when to relax.

Scene One

Have people find a place in an imaginary fishing boat and strike a pose with facial expressions that show how the disciples might have felt after a long day, knowing that they are going home to rest. On signal from the resource leader, all freeze in their position for a few seconds; then relax.

Scene Two

Continue role-playing in the boat. The leader gives instruction to each group to react to the sudden storm that appears. How does each person respond? When all group members are expressing their fears, give the signal to freeze. Signal a thaw.

Scene Three

Continue acting as one would in the midst of a sea storm. The leader calls out that someone is coming toward the boat. Again, react, and freeze! Tell the group that it is Jesus and have them relax in character.

Scene Four

Peter asks if he can walk to Jesus. The other disciples react differently to Peter's request. Freeze.

Scene Five

Peter begins to sink in the water. What expression does he show? How do the disciples react? Freeze.

Scene Six

Peter and Jesus climb into the boat as the others make room. How would the disciples show both their relief that all are safe and their awe that Jesus is really someone special? Freeze. Relax.

Debrief together by asking children to tell what they learned about faith by doing this exercise. Lead into the discussion outlined under Application.

Session 3

An Invitation to Loyalty

| love |
| affection |
| godliness |
| endurance |
| self-control |
| knowledge |
| goodness |
| faith |

Theme: From Loyalty to Betrayal
Bible Texts: John 13:34-38; Mark 14:66-72
Biblical Background: John 13:1-38; John 18:1-11; Luke 22:51; John 19:1—20:1-23
Story Focus: Peter wanted to be a loyal friend to Jesus, but when frightening things that he did not understand began to happen, he denied the friendship. Even though Peter did not pass the loyalty test, Jesus continued to love him.
Faith Focus: It is easy to slip back into old patterns of behaviour when we are faced with new and frightening situations. Jesus continues to love and forgive us even when we do not act like his friend.

Anticipated Outcomes

1. The children will learn parts of 2 Peter 1:5-7.
2. The children will retell the Bible story with clay figures.
3. The children will learn about loyalty between friends.

Materials

- Eight boxes that stack or eight bricks
- "Virtue" words from the memory text written on the boxes (See illustration.)
- 2 Peter 1:5-7 written on chart paper or chalkboard
- Clay, play dough, or plasticine
- Styrofoam meat trays (one per child)
- Plastic bag or plastic wrap for storage

Method

Bible memory

1. Read the verses together.
2. Repeat the verses, this time using the boxes to add the "virtues." See illustration.
3. Distribute the boxes among the children. As the verses are repeated, invite the children to build the virtues in the correct order.

Bible story reinforcement

1. Give each child a clump of clay and a Styrofoam tray. As the children make the clay pliable, review the story together by producing a simple time line of the Bible story.
2. Invite the children to mould people or things that are significant in the story. When completed, have them assemble their objects onto the trays.
3. Have the children pair off to retell the story using their characters.
4. Place the clay creations in plastic bags and set them aside, or have the group leader keep them until the end of the day.

Application

1. Read a book about friends. Any of the stories in the *Frog and Toad* series by Arnold Lobel are appropriate. Another good choice is *Emily and Alice* by Joyce Champion (New York: Gulliver Books, 1993).
2. Form into small groups with one adult and talk about friendships. When have children disappointed their friends by the way they acted, or been let down or hurt by their friends? What have they done about it? What would they tell Peter to do? Encourage respect for each person.
3. Remind the children that Jesus is a friend who will always love them. When we do things that hurt others or Jesus, we can say we are sorry, and Jesus will forgive us.
4. Close with prayer. Invite each person to say aloud, "Thank you, God, for my friend _____." Thank God for giving us friends and showing us how to be a friend.
5. Dismiss the children to their next activity.

Additional ideas

If you have a large group, before class, prepare slips of paper or a list of characters and objects from the Bible story. Either assign or have children choose one character or object to mold from the clay.

Instead of telling the story in pairs, retell the story with group participation. Set up a "stage" area for the story (low table or plastic tablecloth on the floor). Ask for the scenery props to be placed on the stage by the "designers." Then narrate the story, inviting the children to add their pieces at the appropriate times.

At the end of the session, allow the children to take their clay pieces home.

Session 4

An Invitation to Courage

Theme: From Fear to Courage
Bible Text: Acts 2:1-42
Story Focus: At Pentecost, God's Spirit changed Peter from a fearful follower to a courageous leader. Peter was no longer afraid to tell others about Jesus when he realized that the Holy Spirit was helping him.
Faith Focus: When we let God's Holy Spirit live in us, we are given courage to act boldly for Jesus.

Anticipated Outcomes

1. The children will review from memory 2 Peter 1:3, 5-7.
2. The children will review the Bible story using sounds and streamers.
3. The children will learn about facing their fears.

Materials

• Flash cards with the memory verses printed on them (one word or short phrase per card)
• Red, orange, and yellow crepe paper streamers, each about a meter, a yard, in length.

Method

Bible memory

1. Distribute the flash cards.
2. Have the children work together to put the verses in order. Then say the memory work together.
3. Repeat the process. Redistribute the flash cards. See how quickly the verses can be assembled in the correct order.

4. See if the group can say the entire text from memory without the use of the flash cards.

Note: If the group is large, prepare several sets of flash cards and have the groups compete against the clock several times.

Bible story reinforcement

1. Divide the children into three groups.

2. Assign each group a "Pentecost" sound: wind, mumbling noises of a crowd, fire. Have them practise their sounds in their groups. Distribute the streamers so that each person has one.

3. Tell the Pentecost story (Acts 2:1-8, 12-18). Have each group make the sound at the appropriate time.

4. End with all three groups making their sounds at the same time while they wave their streamers.

Application

1. The disciples were afraid of many things when Jesus was no longer with them. They feared being teased or tortured because they followed Jesus, but the Holy Spirit gave them courage to tell others about God and to live boldly for God. In small groups, each with an adult leader, make a list of things that make children fearful. Encourage honesty and respect during this sharing time.

2. Talk about helpful things to do when we are afraid. Use this list to make a litany. Repeat a phrase such as: "When I am afraid of/to _____, I can _____."

3. Close with prayer, inviting each child to tell God silently about her or his biggest fear. Thank God for hearing the prayers of each child. Ask God to give the children courage to face and overcome their fears because God's Spirit is with them all the time to comfort and guide them.

4. Dismiss the children to their next activity.

Additional ideas

1. The story "Dragons and Giants" from *Frog and Toad Together* by Arnold Lobel (New York: Harper and Row, 1971) could be used in the Application time. This story is also in video form.

2. Use the echo pantomime from the Early Childhood section, pages 134-135, as an alternative to the Bible story reinforcement.

Session 5

An Invitation to Acceptance

Theme: From Rejection to Acceptance
Bible Text: Acts 10:1-48
Story Focus: After a vision from God, Peter believed that it was not right for him to be prejudiced against people who were not Jews. All people are accepted by God.
Faith Focus: When we think like God, we value all people as God does.

Anticipated Outcomes

1. The children will review from memory 2 Peter 1:3, 5-7.
2. The children will review the Bible story by means of discussion.
3. The children will learn through role-playing that God loves and accepts all people regardless of skin colour, language, or gender. God wants us to accept people just like Peter did.

Materials

- Copies of the memory work review sheet (page 66), one per child
- Copies of the role-play situations (See page 80.)
- Pens or pencils
- A white bedsheet or tablecloth
- Box(es) with dress-up clothing and simple props to go with the skits
- A camcorder, VCR, and television set (optional)

Method

Bible memory

1. As a final review repeat 2 Peter 1:3, 5-7 together.
2. Give the older children copies of the memory work review sheet and pencils. Younger children may review the text using the flash cards or pic-

tures used earlier in the week.

3. Give the children a few minutes to fill in the blanks. Check it together.

4. Say the text one more time from memory.

Bible story reinforcement

1. Have everyone sit in a circle. In the centre, place a bedsheet or table-cloth that has been folded into fourths. Review the story by asking questions as you unfold the sheet.

a. With the first unfolding, ask what kind of things were in the sheet in Peter's dream. Why did he not appreciate the Spirit's request? (The animals were unclean according to Jewish custom.)

b. With the second unfolding, ask what the animals in the sheet had to do with Cornelius. (Cornelius was a different nationality, a Roman, a person with whom the Jews were not to associate.)

c. With the third unfolding, ask why Peter decided to go to meet Cornelius and tell him about God. (God convinced Peter that God has no favourites.)

d. With the last unfolding, ask how God proved to Peter that everyone belongs in God's family. (The Holy Spirit was given to Cornelius and his friends, proving that people who were not Jews could believe in God too.)

2. Tell the children that the open sheet is a symbol that God accepts each person who wants to be part of God's family, regardless of colour, gender, abilities/disabilities, looks, etc.

Application

1. Divide the children into small groups of four or five.

2. To each group assign a situation that has to do with prejudice or discrimination. Use the role-plays included or design your own situations based on real prejudices faced in your neighbourhood.

3. Give each group time to prepare a skit based on the role-plays.

4. Have each group present their skits to the larger group or to one other group. If you have the equipment, consider videotaping the skits to show them to the entire group later.

5. Ask the children to sit quietly for a few moments and think about times when they have not been kind to people who are different. Remind them that, in God's eyes, everyone is equal. As friends and followers of Jesus, we want to treat everyone as we would like to be treated.

6. Close in prayer, thanking God for being with us and for helping us to see people through God's eyes of love and acceptance.

7. Dismiss the children to their next activity.

Role-play Situations

Distribute the role-plays. Have the groups consider what Peter might have done if he had been faced with a similar situation.

- A group of boys come to the gym for tryouts for the boys' soccer (floor hockey, softball, volleyball) team. This group has played together for a few years, and the boys are also friends. At the gym is a girl who is dressed and ready to try out for the team. She is new to the school. At her previous school she was the star player on the boys' team. The boys know that if she joins the team, one of them will be sidelined. How do they respond to this girl?

- A group of four girls has been together for each other's birthday parties since they have been born. Now they are into sleep-overs each time a birthday comes around. Susan's mother has insisted that for her birthday, Susan must invite Indira, the new girl who lives next door. Her family moved from Pakistan, and she does not have many friends. Susan's mother thinks that by having Indira at Susan's sleep-over, the girls will become close friends. What will the four girls do about Indira?

- It is recess time at school. Two boys and two girls are playing at the basketball stands. A brother and sister approach them. It looks as though they might want to join in the game. The sister and brother have very dark skin, and you notice as they come closer that they are talking to each other in a language that you do not understand. When the girls try to talk with the sister, she does not know what they are saying to her. The boy speaks very broken English. What will this group do?

- It is lunchtime at school. A new person sits down at the table where this group of four always eats together and shares their food. When they see what is in this newcomer's lunch bag, they are surprised. She or he has weird food and wants to share it (something like cookies between two pieces of bread, or another combination of food that is not typical). What does the group do?

- Your family is invited to the neighbour's apartment for dinner. The neighbours have moved from Egypt. You have smelled strong, spicy odours coming from their apartment. The adults in the family are eager to try an Egyptian meal, but the children are not too excited. As the families prepare to eat together, the children realize that there is no food that they recognize. How would your family act in this situation?

Permission is granted to photocopy these role-plays.

Games and Snacks Resource

Games and Snacks Resource

Introduction

Programme

During Games and Snacks the children participate in active games that reinforce the session theme. Each Games and Snacks time has two components: active games and a simple snack. Plan to spend this time out-of-doors if possible. Children will enjoy the fresh air and open space in which to play. Most of the games included can be adapted for indoors. The games can be enjoyed by a wide age range of children.

Eating a simple, nutritious snack provides rest from active learning for the children. Use this time for discussion of the theme, group building, or chatting informally.

Choose snacks that are easy to prepare and that the children will enjoy. Have the Snack coordinator prepare snacks and deliver them to each group at the appropriate times. Nutritious snacks include:
- Cookies with whole grain or wheat flour
- Apple slices with peanut butter
- Celery sticks with a cheese spread
- Pretzels
- Nuts
- Gorp (good old raisins and peanuts)
- Fresh fruits and vegetables
- Popcorn (Session 5)

If you follow the three-way rotation plan, serve the snack at the end of the thirty-minute session for the first group. For the other two groups, serve the snack at the beginning of each session.

Leadership

The Games leader should enjoy leading and participating in active games. If you have a large group of children, plan to have an assistant to run errands, help set up games, and send for snacks. Engage the Group leaders as assistants also. Give them clear instructions and assignments and expect them to participate fully in the games. Children respect adults who are willing to play with them.

Preparation

Read through the entire Games and Snacks Resource. Collect all materials ahead of time. Choose which games you wish to use from the suggestions given. Become familiar with the instructions for each game. Be set up and ready to go before the children come. It may help if you prepare a set of instructions for all the sessions for the Group leaders so that they are aware of what is expected of them.

Reinforcement of the theme

Stories and concepts stay with children when reinforced in a number of ways. Take the time to tell the children how this game fits with the theme. You will find this information listed in the "Anticipated Outcome" section for each session. A brief comment will help the children to identify with the issues faced by Peter. Encourage the children to process the application during snack time. However, keep in mind that this session is meant to be active movement rather than discussion.

Session plans

Session 1

An Invitation to Follow

> **Theme:** From Fisherman to Follower
> **Bible Text:** Mark 1:16-20; Luke 5:1-11
> **Biblical Background:** Mark 1:1-31
> **Story Focus:** Peter was a fisherman who chose to give up his nets and his job to become a follower of Jesus. This was the beginning of a relationship with Jesus that would change his entire life.
> **Faith Focus:** Jesus invites us to become his followers for life.

Games

Rock Call

Anticipated Outcome: Children will need to choose from the many voices calling them to find their own group, just as Peter needed to respond to the invitation of Jesus.

Materials: None

Method

1. Children form groups of up to eight. Each group chooses the name of a rock such as granite, pumice, marble, limestone, diamond, or coal. Each child must remember his or her group's name.

2. A leader makes a list of all the rock names that were chosen.

3. At a signal from the leader, all the children scatter about the playing area and close their eyes.

4. When the leader shouts "Rocky Road," each child calls out loudly the name of their rock. Eyes must remain closed.

5. When the children hear others calling out the same rock name, they must find their way to each other and stay together until all rocks of the same name have found each other. Remind them to keep their eyes closed tightly and try to find their group by listening only.

6. Have members of the "rocky" teams introduce themselves to each other in their small groups. Keep these groups for the game of *Crazy Relay*.

Option: Use the names of different animals instead of rocks. When the children scatter with eyes closed, they make the sound of their animal until they find each other.

Crazy Relay

Anticipated Outcome: The children will follow the directions given by the leader in a relay format. The concept of following instructions closely can be related to the session's theme of Peter's choice to follow Jesus.

Materials

• One large paper bag per team, each containing a set of identical instructions printed on large index cards or construction paper.

Choose from the following ideas for instructions or make up your own "crazy" ideas: Facing your team, give a cheer that includes the name of your team's rock (see *Rock Call*).

• Hop up and down on one foot ten times.
• Make two funny faces at the Games leader.
• Go to the first person on your team and count to ten as fast as you can.
• Put your hands on your head and bow to the last person on your team.
• Go to the shortest person on your team and shake her or his hand.
• Shake your head as you do ten arm circles in front of your team.
• Run backwards around your team's line.
• Take off one shoe and tap it on the ground three times.
• Run on the spot while saying your name ten times.

Method

1. The teams line up behind the designated starting line. An adult leader is seated about four meters, twelve feet, in front of and facing each team. This leader holds the bag with instructions.

2. On signal, the first person from each team runs to the leader, draws a card from the bag, listens while the leader reads the instructions, then follows the instructions while holding the card.

3. When the instructions have been completed, the player returns the card to the leader, runs to the end of the team's line, and sits down. The first team with all players seated is the winner.

The Human Fish Game

Anticipated Outcome: The children will listen to a caller and follow as a particular fish name is named. The connection to the theme is that Jesus called his disciples to join him on his adventure. Some of his disciples were fishermen.

Materials

• Sheets of newspaper, one sheet for each pair of players

Method

1. Arrange sheets of newspaper in a large circle.

2. The children form pairs and sit together on a sheet of newspaper. Each pair chooses the name of a fish, e.g., catfish, salmon, trout, sunfish.

3. Two children are chosen to be "Jesus and his helper." Their newspaper sheet is removed.

4. "Jesus and his helper" move about the circle, calling out names of fish. When the name of a fish chosen by another pair is called, the pair gets up and falls in line behind "Jesus and his helper." Pairs can suggest other fish names to the leaders.

5. "Jesus and his helper" continue to call out names. At any point they

may call out "The net is full!" All remaining seated pairs join the line following "Jesus and his helper."

6. This line continues making its way about the ocean and seashore until "Jesus and his helper" call out "The net is broken!" and everyone must run for the newspaper seats. The pair left out becomes "Jesus and his helper" for the next round.

Rock, Paper, Scissors Tag

Anticipated Outcome: The children will make quick decisions as Peter did when he left his nets immediately to follow Jesus.

Materials
• Rope to determine "home zones" at each end of the playing area

Method

1. Children form two teams. Review the hand symbols for "rock" (closed fist), "paper" (hand extended out flat), and "scissors" (first two fingers extended to form a V). Review the sequence of superiority: paper covers rock, rock breaks scissors, scissors cut paper.

2. Each team decides which symbol to show the opposite team. Then the teams come together, chanting "1, 2, 3, go," at which time all members of the teams show their symbol.

3. The team that loses the draw is chased by the winning team. If any team members are tagged before reaching safety in their home zone, they join the other team. The team with the most players at the end of playtime is the winner.

Snacks (See page 82 for food ideas.)

Take this opportunity to learn everyone's name. Have children say their names and their nicknames. Remind them that Simon was given the nickname Peter which means "Rock." Dismiss the group to the next activity.

Session 2

An Invitation to Faith

Theme: From Faith to Failure to Faith
Bible Text: Matthew 14:22-33
Story Focus: Peter's initial faith in Jesus faltered when he attempted to walk on the water to meet Jesus. After Jesus rescued him, Peter and the disciples believed that Jesus was God's special son.
Faith Focus: When we focus on Jesus, we can do more than we think we can.

Games

Stepping Stones

Anticipated Outcome: The children will participate in an activity that requires close concentration on each step they take to the finish line. They can be reminded that God is our stepping-stone and is guiding us every step of the way.

Materials
- Two large sheets of newspaper for each team (or two large paper footprints)
- Rope for start and finish lines

Method: The object of the game is to be the first team with all members safely across the playing area (8-10 meters, 25-30 feet) and back. This area can be referred to as the "water" to help relive Peter's experiences.

    1. Organize the children into equal teams of about five or six players.

    2. The teams line up at the starting line.

    3. The first player places the sheet of newspaper directly in front of her, putting one foot on it. The second sheet is then placed in front for the second foot. The player must pick up the first piece of paper again, and use it for the third step. The player proceeds across the "water" in this way until the finish line is reached.

    4. The player turns around and repeats the process back to the team and hands the sheets to the next person in line. The player sits down at the end of the line after her journey.

    5. The first team with all players sitting down wins.

Waves in the Water

Anticipated Outcome: The children will simulate the experience of safety in the designated "boat" areas and uncertainty and fear when in the "open water" area.

Material

• Rope for goal lines at both ends of the playing area

Method

1. Choose one person to be the Wave. Divide the rest of the children into two groups.

2. Each group goes behind a goal line at either side of the open area. The area behind the goal lines is the "boat."

3. The Wave stands in the middle of the open area, doing a wave-like motion, then shouts, "Walk on the water!"

4. All the children run to the opposite goal line, trying not to be tagged by the Wave.

5. Any players caught become part of the Wave. They join hands to do the "wave." Then they shout, "Walk on water!"

6. Play continues until all children are part of the Wave.

Rock Tag

Anticipated Outcome: The children find a "safe" spot during a game of tag. This connects to the concept that Peter was safe as long as he kept his eyes on Jesus.

Materials

• Newspapers, old tires, large rocks, or any object that could represent a "safe" spot
• Headband or scarf to designate It

Method

1. Distribute the "safe" objects randomly throughout the playing area.

2. Ask the children to imagine that they are walking on water. The children try to stay away from It. When they are on one of the safe spots, they cannot be tagged by It. Only one person is allowed on a safe spot at a time, so that when someone else comes, the original person in the safe spot must leave. When tagged, the player must put on the headband and become It.

3. Play until several players have had a chance to be It.

4. To make the game more challenging, remove several safe spots during the course of the game.

Variations: Safe zones can be shadows, trees, holding hands with a friend or leader.

Snacks (See page 82.)

Enjoy a snack together. Dismiss the group to its next activity.

Session 3

An Invitation to Loyalty

Theme: From Loyalty to Betrayal
Bible Texts: John 13:34-38; Mark 14:66-72
Biblical Background: John 13:1-38; John 18:1-11; Luke 22:51; John 19:1—20:1-23
Story Focus: Peter wanted to be a loyal friend to Jesus, but when frightening things that he did not understand began to happen, he denied the friendship. Even though Peter did not pass the loyalty test, Jesus continued to love him.
Faith Focus: It is easy to slip back into old patterns of behaviour when we are faced with new and frightening situations. Jesus continues to love and forgive us even when we do not act like his friend.

Games

Bubble Over (an outdoor activity)

Anticipated Outcome: The children will attempt to blow bubbles that will float to a point in the designated distance. The unpredictable nature of the bubbles and the likelihood of needing to stop and start over can be a reminder of Peter's unpredictability and his mistake in his treatment of his friend Jesus.

Materials
- Two large shallow pans
- Two tin cans with both ends removed
- Large plastic container
- Dish-washing soap (higher priced detergents such as "Joy" or "Palmolive" are recommended)
- Glycerine (found in drugstores)
- Ropes for start and finish lines (5 meters, about 15 feet, apart)

Method
1. Mix the bubble solution as follows:
- Fill the large plastic container with 1 litre, about 1 quart, of warm water.

Mix in about 8 tablespoons of soap.
- Add 6-8 tablespoons of glycerine to the mixture.
- Shake well.

2. Pour the bubble solution into the large shallow pans.

3. Divide the group into two teams. Each team has a pan of soap solution and a tin can to use as a bubble-blowing device.

4. One person on each team serves as the bubble blower. Each team huddles behind the starting line with their designated blower. At the signal, the blower blows a bubble. Team members cooperate to blow or fan the bubble across the playing area to the finish line.

5. If the bubble pops, team members must go back to the bubble blower at the starting line and begin again.

6. The first team to get its bubble over the finish line is the champion bubble-blowing team.

Ten-Legged Race

Anticipated Outcome: The children will work together with their teammates to move as one person. Being friends means that we work together toward a common goal.

Materials
- Small towels or scarves
- Ropes for start and finish lines

Method

1. Children join together at the ankles in groups of five.

2. At the signal each group will attempt to walk together towards the goal line. The object is to complete the race with no member of the team falling. As a group competition, try to see who has the least number of falls.

Blanket Ball Toss

Anticipated Outcome: The children will work together as a team to throw a ball back and forth across the net. Cooperation is encouraged.

Materials
- Large beach balls
- Two blankets
- Tennis net or rope

Method

1. Divide the playing area in half. Set up a net in the middle or make a dividing line with a rope.

2. Form teams with six to eight people per team. Each team is given a blanket and a beach ball. Players grasp the edges of their blanket to hold it firm. The beach ball is placed in the middle of the blanket.

3. Have the groups experiment with the ball and blanket until they feel that they have some control of the movement and height of the ball as it is tossed. How many times can they bounce the ball more than a meter, a yard, in height without its falling off the blanket?

4. When the teams feel they have some control over the ball, have them toss the ball back and forth from blanket to blanket.

5. For scoring, count the times the ball can be tossed back and forth successfully without falling off the blanket.

Challenges: Move the teams farther apart for tossing the ball. Have one team toss the ball straight up in the air. The other group must catch the ball.

Partner Activities

Anticipated Outcome: The children will be encouraged to interact positively with a partner to come up with a solution to the problem posed.

Materials
- Large balls
- Blocks
- Pieces of wood measuring 12 x 40 in., 30 x 100 cm.
- Tennis balls

Method
1. Have the children find partners.
2. Invite the children to try the following challenges, or make up your own:
- Can you balance the ball between your bodies without using your hands?
- Can you balance more than one block on some part of your bodies or heads?
- Can you both balance a tennis ball on the piece of wood without using hands?
- Can you walk back-to-back without falling?
- Can you spin each other around?
- Can you do a three-legged walk without falling?
- Can you come up with a stunt and challenge another partner group to do what you can do?

Snacks

Share a snack and dismiss the group to the next activity.

Session 4

An Invitation to Courage

Theme: From Fear to Courage
Bible Text: Acts 2:1-42
Story Focus: At Pentecost, God's Spirit changed Peter from a fearful follower to a courageous leader. Peter was no longer afraid to tell others about Jesus when he realized that the Holy Spirit was helping him.
Faith Focus: When we let God's Holy Spirit live in us, we are given courage to act boldly for Jesus.

Games

Frozen Tag

Anticipated Outcome: The children will participate in a game in which they must act boldly to free a playmate.

Method: Play begins and proceeds as in a regular game of tag except that when tagged, the person caught must "freeze" with arms and legs outstretched. Any other child may "thaw" the person by touching an outstretched arm.

Spread the Spirit

Anticipated Outcome: The children will be reminded that the Holy Spirit can touch us, and that God's love extends to all.

Materials

• Red, yellow, or orange armbands (Spirit symbols) made from lengths of crepe paper or cloth, enough for each person in the group

Method

1. Two children are designated as the leaders. They carry a supply of armbands.
2. At the signal, the group begins to run as in regular tag.
3. When a player is tagged by one of the leaders, the leader shouts "Stop!" and everyone stops running.
4. The leader places or ties the Spirit symbol to the arm of the tagged player. That person becomes a leader who can tag players.

5. Play continues until all players are wearing the Holy Spirit symbol!

Watch for the Spirit

Anticipated Outcome: The children will be reminded that God uses different methods to get people to notice and follow.

Method

1. Each player must have a partner except for one person who becomes It. Partners form a large circle with Partner A standing an arm's length in front of Partner B.

2. It attempts to gain a partner by "inviting" a Partner A to leave her or his partner and become It's partner. It can use a variety of methods that require eye contact: winking, beckoning with a hand, nodding, mouthing the person's name. When a Partner A realizes that she or he is being invited to become It's partner, she or he immediately runs to stand in front of It. Partner B must try to keep Partner A–by reaching out and touching Partner A on the shoulders or waist with both hands. If Partner A slips away without being touched, she or he becomes It's partner. Partner B then becomes the new It.

Note: If the group is large, form more circles. With fewer pairs, there is more action.

Prisoners' Base

Anticipated Outcome: The children will participate in a game in which they must use courage to free their team members.

Materials
- Ropes to delineate the playing field, safe zone, and prisoners' area
- Headbands, different colours for each team
- Frisbee for each team

Method

1. Divide the group into two teams with different coloured headbands.

2. Divide the playing area into two parts with a prisoners' area cordoned off in the corner of each end. In the opposite corner place the team's Frisbee.

3. Each team stands in the safe zone of its playing area. (See illustration.)

4. At the signal, teams advance toward each other's territory to capture the opponent's Frisbee and take it to their own safe zone.

5. When a person is tagged by a member of the opposite team, that person is escorted to the opponent's prison and remains there until freed by one of her or his own teammates.

6. Any member may free a prisoner by tagging her or him. This pair is allowed free passage to its own safe zone.

7. The game is over when any of the following occurs: the leader calls time, a Frisbee is captured, all the members of one team are in prison.

Snacks

Share a snack and dismiss the group to the next activity.

Session 5

An Invitation to Acceptance

Theme: From Rejection to Acceptance
Bible Text: Acts 10:1-48
Story Focus: After a vision from God, Peter believed that it was not right for him to be prejudiced against people who were not Jews. All people are equally accepted by God.
Faith Focus: When we think like God, we value all people as God does.

Games

Anticipated Outcomes: The children will participate in games that originate in other cultures as a way of understanding and appreciating the heritage of other people.

Freeze

Explanation: This game comes from the Northern Cheyenne tribe. Children will move with the beat to the drum, then stop and freeze when the music stops.
Materials
• Drum or bucket
• Wooden spoon or stick
Method
  1. Choose a leader who has a good sense of rhythm. Give this person a drum or bucket and wooden spoon, anything that can tap out a loud beat.
  2. As the drummer beats out a rhythm, the children jump or move to the beat. When the beat is faster, the children move faster.
  3. At any time the drummer may stop beating the drum. At that moment, all the dancers must freeze their movements until the drummer begins again.
  4. Dancers thaw out and continue to move when the drum beats again.
  5. If desired, the drummer can choose a "frozen" person to replace her or him. This person can be the one who is the best frozen, or the one who was the last to freeze, or someone of personal choice.

Chopstick Relay

Explanation: This game comes from Asian sources. Children must use chopsticks to transfer peanuts from one place to another.

Materials
- Chairs, one per team
- Bowls (one per team) filled with unshelled peanuts or large, dried beans
- Chopsticks, one set per team

Method

1. Set up the relay course. At the starting end, place a bowl filled with unshelled peanuts or large, dried beans on a chair. Set up enough chairs with bowls so that each team has its own. Place two chopsticks in the bowl. Set up chairs directly across from the starting chair, at a distance of about 12 to 15 feet, 4 meters. On these chairs, set an empty bowl.

2. Form into teams that have the same number of children. If the teams are uneven, have one or two children repeat the activity on their line. Have the children line up behind the chair with the chopsticks and peanuts.

3. On the word "go," the first person from each team must transport one peanut from the full bowl to the empty bowl using the chopsticks in one hand. When the peanut is deposited in the second bowl, the person will run back to her or his line and hand the chopsticks to the next person.

4. If a peanut is dropped, the person returns to the bowl to try again.

5. After everyone has had a turn, eat the peanuts together. Or to show transformational thinking, the leader may wish to give the peanuts to the group that took the longest time to complete the relay.

Bucket Brigade Relay (an outdoor activity)

Explanation: This game can remind children of the luxury of water availability. In Cambodia, people carry their water in buckets from a stream or well close by. The object of the game is to transfer water from one bucket to the other without losing it all or getting too wet!

Materials
- Chairs, one per team
- Plastic buckets with handles, two per team
- Long poles, one per team
- Tub filled with water

Method

1. Set up a relay course about 10 feet, 3 meters, from the starting line to a chair or marker.

2. Form into teams. Each team will have two plastic buckets with handles and a long pole, such as a broom handle. Set up a tub with water to fill the buckets at the starting line.

3. On the starting signal, the first person will go to the tub of water, fill both buckets halfway, insert the pole through the handles, and carry the pails over the shoulders around the chair and back to the starting line. There she or he will empty the water into the tub. The next person starts all over again.

4. The game is over when each person has filled the bucket, carried the water, and emptied the water again.

Note: As leader, you will have to make some decisions on what happens when water is spilled on the ground or on the children. Have some fun with this game.

It would be good to talk with the children about the reality of this activity for many children in the world. What would life be like if children had to carry all the water they use in a day from a stream a distance from their home?

Additional games

Stone Catch

This game is often played by children in Lesotho, Africa, but also by old grannies. Some of the grannies are known as the champions in their part of the village.

Collect a handful of small stones about 1/2 inches, 1.25 centimeters, in diameter. Pick up as many as you can hold in one hand and throw them about 8-10 inches, 20-25 centimeters, in the air. Try to catch as many as possible on the back of one hand. Then, toss the stones up again and catch as many as possible in the palm of the same hand. Find out who can catch the most stones this way.

Variations: Clap your hands quickly after the stones are thrown into the air, then catch the stones. Or, have a pile of extra stones close by. After you throw the stones in your hand up into the air, pick up as many stones as you can from the extra pile before you catch the stones you threw into the air.

Try playing *Stone Catch* with several friends. Sing and clap together as you throw the stones up into the air and try to catch them.

If there are children in your group from other cultures, invite them to lead the group in some of their favourite games.

Check your local library for books that contains games from other cultures.

1. *Handbook of American Indian Games,* Allan and Paulette Macfarlan (General Publishing Company, 1985).

2. *International Playtime: Classroom Games and Dances from Around the World,* Wayne E. Nelson (Carthage, Ill.: Paramount Communications, Fearon Teacher Aids, 1992).

3. *Neighbors Near and Far* (Newton, Kans.: Faith & Life Press, 1987-89).

All games for Session 5 are taken from *Neighbors Near and Far* (Faith & Life Press, 1988-89). Used by permission.

Snacks

Popcorn is a North American treat. Offer popcorn with a variety of toppings: chili powder, seasoned salt, garlic salt, parmesan cheese, cinnamon and sugar mixture. Check your local health food store for additional flavours.

To serve the popcorn, place a napkin inside a drinking cup. Children put the popcorn into the cup, shake on the topping, and eat. When finished, have them remove the napkin. Serve the juice in the cup.

Dismiss the group to the next activity.

Make
and Take
Resource

Make and Take Resource

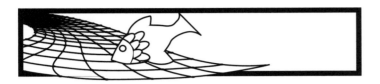

Introduction

Programme

During Make and Take the children do art or craft activities that reinforce the daily themes. The session is designed for thirty minutes with five minutes travel time to the next activity. These items can be taken home as a reminder of Peter's story and its application to the child's life.

Leadership

The leader should enjoy working in a creative environment that encourages children to make response items that are personal and reflect their understanding of the Bible story. Do not expect uniform, perfect crafts, but help children express the themes in personal ways through the media of arts and crafts.

   If your group is larger than eight children, work together with an assistant. Also ask the Group leaders to help you. Give them clear instructions. Expect them to participate. Encourage them to continue to build on the theme by relating the activity to the Bible story drama and other activities that have been done so far.

Preparation

Read through the entire Make and Take Resource. Beforehand, collect all materials necessary for each craft activity. Take the time to make each craft so that you know if the instructions are clear, how long it will take, and what it should look like. Have a sample for the children to see. If you substitute a craft, be sure that the replacement activity appropriately expresses the theme.

   Prepare a set of instructions on chart paper so that children and Group leaders can follow along as they work.

   Allow for cleanup time so that the next groups will not have to wait. Set up an area in the room for storing crafts until the end of the day. Label each craft with the child's name and the name of the group.

Reinforcement of the theme

Stories and concepts stay with the children when reinforced in a number of ways. Take the time to tell the children how the craft activity fits with the theme. Check the "Anticipated Outcomes" for each session, pages 100-110. A brief comment will help the children connect the craft with the session theme.

Additional ideas

Some children complete their craft activities more quickly than others. Set up a corner of your craft area for a mural. Print the title of the session's story or theme and invite children to draw pictures on the mural when they finish their crafts. Have available markers, crayons, and/or paints. Set out containers with different colours of poster paint. Have small sponges on hand. Encourage the children to illustrate themselves in the picture, draw background scenes, or add present-day characters. Invite the children to tell a Group leader about their illustrations.

Session plans

Session 1

An Invitation to Follow

Theme: From Fisherman to Follower
Bible Text: Mark 1:16-20; Luke 5:1-11
Biblical Background: Mark 1:1-31
Story Focus: Peter was a fisherman who chose to give up his nets and his job to become a follower of Jesus. This was the beginning of a relationship with Jesus that would change his entire life.
Faith Focus: Jesus invites us to become his followers for life.

Pet Rocks

Anticipated Outcome: The children will make a pet rock to remind them of Simon's new name and Jesus' belief that Peter had rocklike qualities.

Materials

- Small stones of various sizes, colours, shapes, and textures
- Acrylic paints
- Small brushes and brush cleaner
- Odds and ends (cotton balls, bits of fabric, feathers)
- Movable plastic eyes
- Glue guns and transparent glue sticks
- Felt pieces
- Scissors

Method

1. Choose a stone suitable for the main part of your pet rock. Choose smaller stones for legs, arms, head, etc.

2. Decide on the shape, then glue the stones together.

3. Decorate your pet rock with eyes, odds and ends, and paint. Allow time for it to dry.

4. Glue a small piece of felt to the bottom of the rock to prevent scratching on wood surfaces.

5. The children should print their names onto pieces of masking tape and attach tape to the felt bottom.

6. Set rocks aside until the end of the day.

Allow time for cleanup. Engage the help of everyone. Dismiss the group to their next activity.

Alternative suggestions

1. Make stone paperweights by gluing small stones (size of a jelly bean) to a piece of corkboard, wood, or cardboard. Paint the stones different colours. When the glue and paint are dry, cover each stone with shellac. Allow stones to dry.

2. Make stone necklaces, pins, or keychains. Purchase polished stones in a variety of shapes and sizes. You will need to purchase jewelry clasps that can be glued to the stone. Check your local craft store. Use braided thread, leather strips, or chain for the necklace. Key chain holders can be purchased at a craft store also.

Session 2

An Invitation to Faith

Theme: From Faith to Failure to Faith
Bible Text: Matthew 14:22-33
Story Focus: Peter's initial faith in Jesus faltered when he attempted to walk on the water to meet Jesus. After Jesus rescued him, Peter and the disciples believed that Jesus was God's special son.
Faith Focus: When we focus on Jesus, we can do more than we think we can.

Sinking Peter Puppet

Anticipated Outcome: The children will make a puppet as a reminder that Peter needed to keep his eyes on Jesus in order to walk on the water. The puppet will remind them that Jesus was a trustworthy friend.

Materials

- One wooden dowel (1/4 x 12 in., .62 x 30 cm.) per person
- One blue cardboard cone (4 in., 10 cm., long and 2 1/2 in., 6.25 cm., in diameter) per person (See page 00.)
- One white Styrofoam ball (1 to 1 1/4 in., 2.5 to 3 cm., in diameter) per person
- Yarn, felt, ribbon, and lace scraps
- White glue
- White broadcloth cloaks (see pattern, page 105), one per person
- Small paper or cloth fish, or fish seals (optional)
- Round wooden beads (optional), one per person

Method

1. Make the cone from heavy blue bristol board (see pattern) or purchase cones from a craft store. (Sewing thread bases can be used as an alternative.)

2. Glue the bottom of the cloak over the outside edge of the cone at the wide end. Cover the glued seam with a piece of ribbon or lace to make a neater finish.

3. Insert the dowel through the narrow end of the cone until the end of the dowel is at the top of the cloak's neck.

4. Make a hole in the Styrofoam ball just large enough to insert the dowel.

5. Place a dab of white glue on the neck end of the dowel and insert it into the hole in the ball. Let it dry for a few minutes.

6. Add facial features and hair to the ball.

7. Print the child's name on the inside of the cone.

8. Slide the cone up and down the dowel to make Peter sink or walk on water.

Options
• Glue small fish to the cone.
• Glue a round bead to the end of the dowel at the bottom as a safety feature. Allow for cleanup time and dismiss the group to their next activity.

Alternative suggestions
Recycled Two-litre Pop Bottles

1. Terrarium: Make a real rock garden in a pop bottle. Cut the bottle open just above the bottom ridge. Fill the base with potting soil and a slip from an ivy plant or other appropriate plant that has been rooted beforehand. Add some small painted stones, seashells, or aquarium gravel. Push the top of the bottle inside the bottom part, being careful not to dislodge the plant. Children will be able to watch the plant grow. It will be a reminder that our faith in God is a growing, alive faith that takes time and nourishment to grow strong and healthy. (See illustration.)

Option: Cut out a piece of "florist oasis" (Styrofoam-like material) to fit the bottom of the bottle. Stick in dried or artificial flowers, or twigs, moss, and outdoor materials.

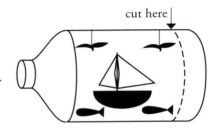

cut here

2. Boat in a Bottle: Cut the pop bottle open just above the bottom ridge. Make a small boat out of bristol board, using cloth scraps for the sail. Attach the boat to the "bottom" of the bottle that is turned on its side. Surround the boat and bottle bottom with crumpled blue tissue paper. Add pictures of birds and sea creatures. Attach birds to the "top" with white thread or fishing line and clear tape. Add sea creatures in among the blue tissue paper waves. (See illustration.)

Sinking Peter Puppet
Cone Pattern

B
A

C

Glue this area.

Trace around pattern for the cone.
Use heavy blue bristol board.
Cut out pattern.
Make the cone by taping or stapling **A** to **B**.
Cut off the tip of the cone (**C**).

C — — — — — — — — — — — — — — — — — B

A

Permission is granted to photocopy this page.

Sinking Peter Puppet

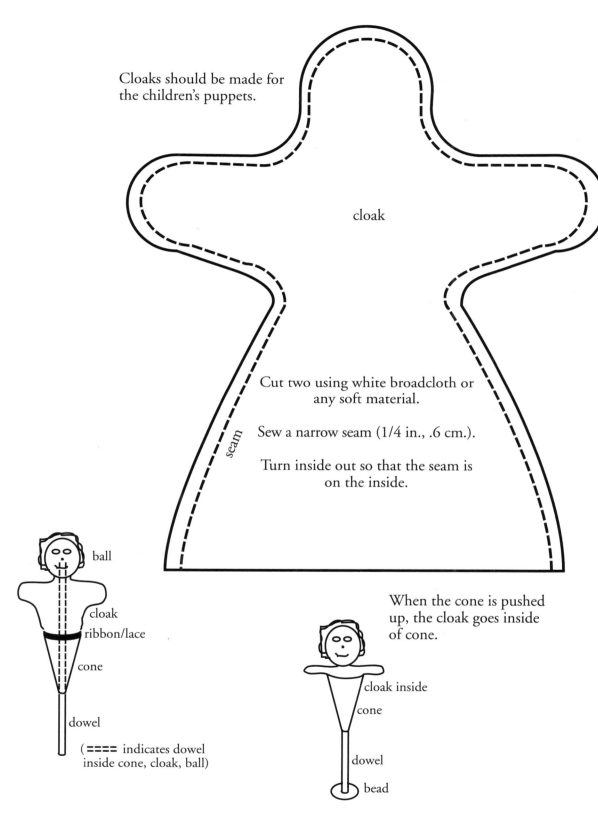

Cloaks should be made for the children's puppets.

cloak

Cut two using white broadcloth or any soft material.

Sew a narrow seam (1/4 in., .6 cm.).

Turn inside out so that the seam is on the inside.

seam

ball

cloak

ribbon/lace

cone

dowel

(==== indicates dowel inside cone, cloak, ball)

When the cone is pushed up, the cloak goes inside of cone.

cloak inside

cone

dowel

bead

Session 3

An Invitation to Loyalty

Theme: From Loyalty to Betrayal
Bible Texts: John 13:34-38, Mark 14:66-72
Biblical Background: John 13:1-38; John 18:1-11; Luke 22:51; John 19:1—20:1-23
Story Focus: Peter wanted to be a loyal friend to Jesus, but when frightening things that he did not understand began to happen, he denied the friendship. Even though Peter did not pass the loyalty test, Jesus continued to love him.
Faith Focus: It is easy to slip back into old patterns of behaviour when we are faced with new and frightening situations. Jesus continues to love and forgive us even when we do not act like his friend.

Pliers Painting

Anticipated Outcome: The children will cooperate to make friendship cards as a way of learning that cooperation builds trust between friends.
Materials
- Pliers (one for every two children)
- Folded pieces of construction paper
- Variety of small hardware (nuts, bolts, screws, nails)
- Tempera paints
- Containers for paints
Method
1. Give each pair of children one pair of pliers and two pieces of construction paper.
2. Each child holds onto one handle of the pliers. Use the pliers to pick up a piece of hardware, dip it into the paint, and press it on the paper to make a design on the card.
3. Each pair should make at least two cards. When the paint dries, write a message of friendship on the inside of the card.
4. Encourage the children to give away the card to a friend.
   Clean up and dismiss the group to the next activity.

Alternative activities

Friendship Pennant or Place Mat

Anticipated Outcome: The children will make a pennant or place mat with pictures or a brief message to remind them that being a good friend requires effort and love, but it is very rewarding.

Materials

- Coloured bristol board or construction paper
- Felt pieces
- Glue
- Scissors
- Dowels for pennants
- Adhesive-backed clear plastic
- Odds and ends for decorating
- Magazines (checked for suitability)
- 2 or 3 in., 5 or 7.5 cm., sizes of the letters of the alphabet for tracing (optional)

Method for a Pennant

1. Have children choose a friendship message they wish to place on the pennant. Suggestions are: A friend cares, Jesus is my friend, A friend loves at all times.

2. Cut out or draw/trace letters for the message from paper or felt.

3. Cut out the pennant shape, large enough to accommodate the printed message. If you choose to use dowelling, allow for extra felt or paper to be wrapped around it.

4. Glue the lettering securely into place.

5. Add odds and ends to decorate the pennant.

6. Attach the dowel with staples or glue.

Method for a Place Mat

1. Divide a piece of bristol board into four pieces.

2. Distribute magazines.

3. Have children find pictures that illustrate friendship. Tear out these pictures.

4. Cut around the pictures to make interesting shapes. Glue onto the bristol board so that the pictures overlap.

5. Cut out letters from magazines or from coloured paper to make a message.

6. Glue the message on top of the pictures or as a heading.

7. Cover the entire picture with adhesive-backed plastic. Cut out a section about 2 inches, 5 centimeters, larger than the piece of bristol board. Carefully remove the backing and place the picture face down onto the sticky plastic.

Note: This may require adult assistance. It is easy for the plastic to crease. It is difficult to remove the plastic from the paper. The Make and Take leader or Group leaders can do this part of the craft at another time.

Friendship Bead Necklace

Younger children might enjoy making a friendship bead necklace out of strips of magazine or construction paper. Check instructions in Early Childhood, page 129.

Friendship Bracelet

A friendship bracelet can be made using coloured plastic gimp or embroidery thread. Instructions and materials for lacing gimp and knotting thread can be found in craft stores. These bracelets will take longer to complete, but children will be able to learn how to do the lacing/knotting so that it can be completed at home.

Session 4

An Invitation to Courage

Theme: From Fear to Courage
Bible Text: Acts 2:1-42
Story Focus: At Pentecost, God's Spirit changed Peter from a fearful follower to a courageous leader. Peter was no longer afraid to tell others about Jesus when he realized that the Holy Spirit was helping him.
Faith Focus: When we let God's Holy Spirit live in us, we are given courage to act boldly for Jesus.

Mobile

Anticipated Outcome: A mobile with appropriate symbols will remind the children of this special event of Pentecost. The symbols of the Holy Spirit can assure the children that God's Spirit gives them courage.

Materials
• Coat hangers or aluminum plates
• Various lengths of wire, yarn, or fishing line
• Construction paper or felt
• Scissors, glue, markers, tape, wire cutters (dependent upon other materials chosen above)

Method
1. Choose the style of mobile hanger.
2. Make symbols of the Holy Spirit: wind, flame, tongue, dove, etc. These can be drawn on paper or cut from felt or paper.
3. Punch holes for attaching mobile pieces. Tie one end of the yarn to the symbol and the other to the mobile holder. If you have chosen to use the aluminum plates, have the holes punched beforehand.

Clean up together and dismiss the group to their next activity.

Alternative activities

Wind Chimes

Materials

- Plastic containers (2 cups, 500 ml.), one per person
- Smooth, round lids from frozen juice cans (ones that do not require a can opener), five per person
- Fishing line
- Nails
- Permanent markers

Method

1. Before the session, spray paint the juice can lids on both sides. Punch holes in the lids for hanging.

2. Make symbols of the Holy Spirit such as wind, flame, or dove on each of the juice lids. Use permanent markers or the sharp end of a nail to make the symbol.

3. Using the nail, make holes around the edge of the plastic container, one for each "chime."

4. Make two holes at the centre of the bottom of the container so that it will hang.

5. Assemble the chimes. Attach each lid to the container, using fishing line. Thread a length of fishing line through the two holes in the bottom and tie together.

6. Hang outside in the breeze as a reminder of the presence of God's Spirit.

Alternative Mobile Using a Plastic Bottle

Materials

- Three rings per person (each ring about a 3/4 in., 2 cm., width cut from the centre of a two-litre plastic pop bottle or similar bottle)
- Small metal or plastic ring
- Button
- String
- Paper punch
- Paper, cardboard, or Styrofoam meat trays
- Scissors, tape

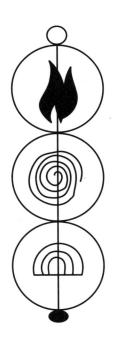

Method

1. Cut the rings from the plastic bottle.
2. Punch holes to thread the string.
3. Tie one end of the string to the small metal or plastic ring and attach to the first larger ring. String through the other two circles. (See illustration.) Fasten the string at the bottom, using a button. The string will hold the mobile together.

4. Using paper or meat trays, cut out three symbols of the Holy Spirit or pictures that remind the children of today's story.

5. Attach each symbol to the string in the circles, using clear tape.

Session 5

An Invitation to Acceptance

Theme: From Rejection to Acceptance
Bible Text: Acts 10:1-48
Story Focus: After a vision from God, Peter believed that it was not right for him to be prejudiced against persons who were not Jews. All people are equally accepted by God.
Faith Focus: When we think like God, we value all people as God does.

Butterfly

Anticipated Outcome: Few things illustrate change as beautifully as the change from a caterpillar to a butterfly. The theme of change has been highlighted in the stories about Peter. The children will be reminded that Jesus, our friend, can change us into something more special that we can even imagine!

    Note: If possible, set up separate tables and a set of instructions for each of the following butterfly designs. Allow the children to choose the kind of butterfly that will remind them of being changed by God. You may wish to assign a different activity to each of the group leaders to prepare and lead.

Butterfly #1
Materials
- Piece of black construction paper 12 x 18 in., 30 x 45 cm., one per child
- Scissors
- Glue
- Tissue paper or coloured cellophane
- White chalk or white pencil crayons

Method
    1. Fold the construction paper in half so that it is 9 x 12 inches, 22.5 x 30 centimeters.

    2. At the fold, draw half of a butterfly's body, one eye, and one antenna. Draw front and back wings towards the open side of the fold.

    3. With the chalk draw circles, ovals, or irregular shapes on the wings of

the butterfly.

4. Carefully cut out the butterfly outline and the shapes while keeping the paper folded in order to have identical shapes.

5. Unfold the paper.

6. Cut pieces of coloured tissue paper to cover the spaces in the wings. Using the same colour for matching spaces on each side of the body, glue the tissue paper on the underside of the black paper.

Butterfly #2
Materials
- Colourful glossy pages from magazines
- Black permanent markers
- Black pipe cleaner pieces (each 6 in., 15 cm., in length)
- Copies of the wing patterns in different sizes (See page 112.)

Method
1. Prepare the patterns by tracing onto cardboard. Make several sizes of the pattern by enlarging and decreasing the size of both wing patterns. Have enough patterns so that each child will have one set.

2. Have the children find brightly coloured pages from glossy magazines. Place the patterns on the magazine page and trace around them with a black marker.

3. Cut out the wings at the outside edge of the black line.

4. Make one 1/4 inch, .62 centimeter, accordion-pleat fold toward the outer edges on each of the wings.

5. Fold the pipe cleaner in half. Twist 1/2 inches, 1.25 centimeters, up from the fold to form the lower body.

6. Place the upper wing beside the lower wing and pinch the two together at the centre of the pleats. Secure with the next part of the pipe cleaner.

7. Twist the remaining portion of the pipe cleaner into the shape of the antennae.

Options
- To make a magnet of the butterfly, attach a small piece of magnetic tape to the pipe-cleaner body.
- To make it into a houseplant decoration, tape the body of the butterfly to a piece of dowel or a plastic straw and insert it into the soil in the pot.
  Clean up and dismiss the group to the next activity.

Alternative activities

Fish Craft

Some children enjoy oragami paper folding. Consider making several oragami fish as a symbol of following Jesus then and now. Paper folding is an ancient art of the Japanese culture.

For directions to make an oragami fish see *Becoming God's Peacemakers*, Living Stones Collection, page 75 (Newton, Kans.: Faith & Life Press, 1992). Or find instructions for oragami in the library or a local craft store. If possible, invite a craftsperson skilled in the art to demonstrate and teach.

Wing Patterns

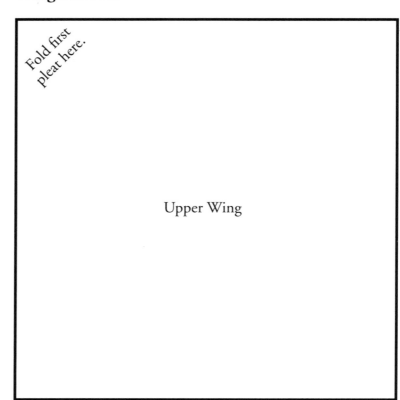

Fold first
pleat here.

Upper Wing

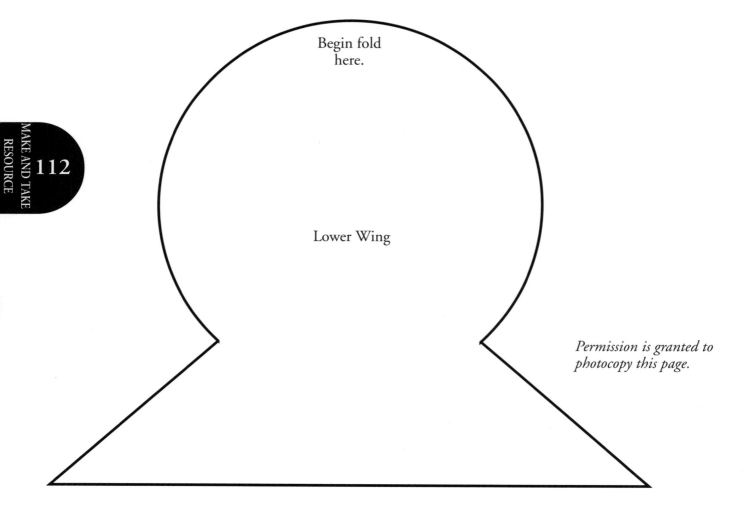

Begin fold
here.

Lower Wing

*Permission is granted to
photocopy this page.*

Early Childhood

Early Childhood Introduction

This curriculum is for children ages three, four, and five, pre-kindergarten and kindergarten age levels. Children who have completed kindergarten are considered part of the broadly graded track (page 24). If children who have completed kindergarten are included in early childhood, some adaptations will need to be made to keep the material challenging for them.

Alter the length and order of the sessions to suit your needs. Choose which activities you will omit for a shorter programme. Younger children may need more playtime while older children could use more "talk" time.

Groupings

Divide into several groups if you have a large group of children. Each group should have a teacher and Group leader. Groups may combine three- four- and five-year-olds in the same group or be separated by ages.

Combine the children for singing, the Bible story, and group games. Consider a rotation schedule (see pages 20-21), or have each group work on its own schedule with each teacher and Group leader providing total leadership for crafts, story reinforcements, etc.

Give each group a name. Different fish names would be appropriate. Or choose colours.

Group leaders

Read the Group leader's section (pages 14-21) to find out what is expected. Adapt the information to fit the early childhood ages.

Special items

Accordion activity booklet

Each session has a page for the children to colour. Make enough copies so each child has one. In Session 4, assemble the booklet so that the children can complete it the next day.

To assemble, glue the pictures to coloured construction paper. Tape the pages together to form a foldout booklet. Add the construction paper page for Session 5 so that when the children complete the picture, they can glue it onto the last page of the accordion book. See illustration.

Options
• Make a title page and glue to reverse side of Session 1 page. The title page is visible only when the book is closed.
• Add one page at the end. Shift drawings one page to the right. Put title page on left-handed page so it is visible when the book is displayed.

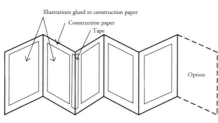

Illustrations glued to construction paper

Construction paper

Tape

Option

Tabletop setting

Make a tabletop setting that children can use to retell the story.

Supplies
- A roll of table paper or enough brown grocery bags (cut open with the bottom cut out) taped together to cover the table
- Blocks
- Empty toilet-tissue rolls
- Play dough
- Green tissue paper
- Coloured aquarium stones
- Crayons, or markers

Method
1. Cover the table with paper.
2. Using crayons or markers, draw a pathway to the seaside.
3. Make 1 1/2 inch, 3.75 centimeter, slits at one end of the toilet-tissue rolls. Have children make trees by inserting green tissue paper into the ends.
4. Distribute play dough. Have some children make people, others make fish, boats, and other seaside items.
5. Use blocks to make a house by the sea.
6. Apply glue to the "sea" area of the table top, then cover with blue aquarium stones or coloured gravel to represent the water.
7. When the scene is in place, retell the story, using the play-dough figures.

Memory work suggestions

The memory text is 2 Peter 1:3, 5-7. See Early Childhood Resources, pages 143-144, for ideas on Bible memorization. Short Bible verses appear on the daily take-home pages. These verses may be used in Memory work instead of the longer text.

Puppet plays

Puppet plays are included in Early Childhood Resources, pages 146-151. Instructions for making puppets are found on page ??. Ask people to rehearse the plays so they can be presented effectively. Junior youth children may be willing to help prepare and present these puppet stories. A group of teenagers or some of your group leaders could be assigned this responsibility.

Closing celebration

Invite the families to join the group for a brief closing celebration. Plan an informal and relaxed time. Meet and greet the important adults in the children's lives. Have the children sing favourite songs (including the theme song), repeat the memory verses, and tell about their week. You may wish to videotape some of the activities each day and show them to parents as a summary of the week's activities. Enjoy a simple snack together.

If there are families who do not have a church home, use this opportunity to invite them to participate in the church life of your congregation. Have brochures or information about your church available.

Enjoy the programme

Vacation Bible school is meant to be enjoyed by children and their adult leaders. If you are having a good time learning about Peter and Jesus, the children will enjoy themselves. Remember, VBS is about building relationships, modelling Christian discipleship, and learning about God's love for each one

of us. Jesus Christ can transform us. Give the Holy Spirit an opportunity to change you through your time together with Simon Peter and the children.

Session plan

These materials are intended for a two-and-three-quarter-hour programme. Make adjustments to suit your time frame.

Gather and Greet (15 minutes)

Collect the children's offering, distribute name tags, take attendance, and conduct group-building activities.

Worship (30 minutes)

Sing songs, review memory work, and tell the Bible story for the day.

A Bible story has been included for each day. Consider varying the way you present the story. Try puppets, story figures, acting out the story, or having older youth present it. If the same person tells the story, try presenting it in the third person or become "Peter" and relate his experiences in the first person.

Use the music from Early Childhood Resources (pages 156-159) for worship. Add other favourites the children already know. Use music at other times throughout the session for a change of pace or to indicate the next activity.

Respond (35 minutes)

1. Reinforce the story each day in a variety of ways: use a tabletop setting (see page 115) that children can build together; provide dress-up clothing and simple props so the children can act out the story.

2. Include a "talk time" for children to relate to the Bible story at an appropriate age level. Use the questions to talk about the story. Help the children continue thinking about the story.

3. Make an accordion-style activity booklet with pictures that illustrate the Bible story. Use the pictures provided with each session to form the accordion activity book. The children will have daily reminders of the story of Peter to take home.

Make-It (35 minutes)

Each craft is related to the session theme. Collect the supplies ahead of time. Make a sample of the craft so you know what parts need teacher assistance and what things the children can do on their own.

Games and Snacks (35 minutes)

Play games in a large room or outside, if possible. The games relate to the theme.

Provide simple nutritional snacks each day. Have puzzles, toys, and activities available for free playtime.

Gather and Bless (15 minutes)

Present the puppet play; sing; say a closing blessing; collect the items to take home; and give instructions for the next day.

Each session contains a puppet play. The puppet plays are stories that reinforce each theme. Five animal puppets are the characters. See Early Childhood Resources, page 145-155, for the plays and patterns for sock puppets.

Session plans

Session 1

Invitation to Follow: From Fisherman to Follower

> **Bible Text:** Mark 1:16-20; Luke 5:1-11
> **Biblical Background:** Mark 1:1-31
> **Story Focus:** Peter was a fisherman who chose to give up his nets and his job to become a follower of Jesus. This was the beginning of a relationship with Jesus that would change his entire life.
> **Faith Focus:** Jesus invites us to become his followers for life.

Gather and Greet

Welcome all the children. Make name tags to help you remember each child's name. Be sure each child feels comfortable and included. Engage them in a play centre or some activity. Collect offering and take attendance.

Worship

1. Sing together. Start with songs that may be familiar to most children from Sunday school. Choose from the following songs. (See Early Childhood Resources, pages 156-159.) Consider the song "Together" as your theme song for worship each day.

"Together"
"Hallelujah Ballad–Peter"
"Fisherman Peter" (Worship Resource, page 55)
"Jesus and His Friends"

2. Present the Bible story. Remember that Bible stories are most effective when told rather than read.

Simon and his friends were taking care of their fishing nets. They used big nets to scoop up the fish. Today they were tired because they had been in their boats fishing all night long and had not caught any fish! Jesus came along and told them to get back into the boat and try some more fishing. Simon, Andrew, and Jesus got into the boat. [*Place one boat in the water. Children put three pipe-cleaner figures into the plastic boat.*]

They went further out into the lake. Then Jesus told them to put their nets into the water again. Simon and the others did not want to fish any more because they thought they would not catch anything anyway. Jesus finally got them to try again. So they put their net into the water. [*Let the children work together to catch fish.*] There were so many fish that they called the other fishermen to help them. [*Use second boat to help out.*]

Then Jesus said to Simon, "You have been catching *fish*. Now I want you to come with me and catch *people*." Simon thought maybe Jesus was teasing him–he knew he couldn't catch people with nets.

Jesus said, "No, Simon, you don't use nets. You tell people who I am and that I want to be friends with them. Another thing, Simon, I want to give you a new name. I'm going to call you Peter. 'Peter' means 'rock,' and I want you to be like a rock, strong and firm. Peter, will you come with me?"

Peter got right out of the boat and went with Jesus. So did his friend Andrew. They wanted to be Jesus' friends.

3. Pray together. "Dear God, thank you for Jesus and his friend Simon Peter. We want to be your friend, too. Amen." Pray the prayer in phrases, inviting children to repeat after you.

Respond

1. Reinforce the Bible story. Retell the story using objects and the children's help. You may wish to tell the story a few times so that several children can participate by adding the props at the appropriate times.

Supplies

- Two plastic boats made from apple-cider jugs (See illustration.)
- Pipe cleaners to make at least four fishermen and Jesus figures to place in the boat
- Two nets to "catch" fish (use the netting that can be found in the packaging of fruit)
- Piece of string woven around the edge of the netting to serve as a drawstring for the fish that are caught
- Small plastic or paper fish
- Large tub of water for the lake

2. Talk about the story after the children have participated in retelling it several times.
- How was Simon Peter supposed to "catch" people?
- What is a rock like? (You may wish to show a variety of stones that differ in shape, texture, and size.)
- How was "Peter" going to be like a rock?
- How can we choose to be friends of Jesus?

3. Begin making the Accordion Activity Booklet. Distribute the page for Session 1 (page 121) and crayons. Have the children colour the picture. Place the child's name on the back of the page. Set aside until Session 4. See Information on page 114 for instructions.

Discard portion
with handle

Make-It

Choose one of the following ideas:

1. Make a fishing boat and net.

Supplies

- 16 oz., 500-ml., cardboard cream containers, cut in half to form two boats
- Netting: orange or onion bags, or cheesecloth cut into 8 x 10 in., 20 x 25 cm., pieces
- Gimp, shoelaces, or heavy string (3-foot, 1-meter, length per child)

Instructions

a. Cut cream containers in half lengthwise for two boats. Glue or staple shut the pour spout, if necessary. Each person receives one boat.

b. To make netting: Distribute a piece of netting to each person and a length of gimp. Have children "sew" around the four edges of netting in approximately one-inch stitches. A needle is not necessary. Tie gimp ends together. Pull at two opposite corners to gather and make handles.

Use the boat and net for the memory verse game. Let the children take them home with the fish at the end of the day.

2. Make painted rocks.

Supplies

- Smooth stones
- Acrylic paints and paint brushes.

Instructions:

Children paint a stone as a reminder of Peter's new name. Use the painted rock as a paperweight. See page 101 for additional instructions and ideas.

Games and Snacks

1. Play *Fishing Memory Game.*

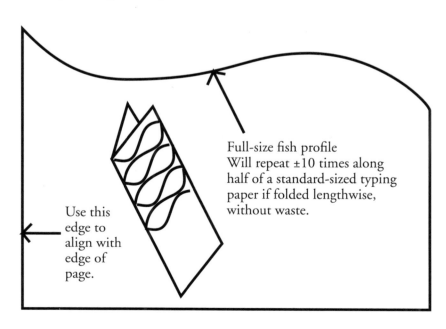

Use this edge to align with edge of page.

Full-size fish profile
Will repeat ±10 times along half of a standard-sized typing paper if folded lengthwise, without waste.

Supplies

- Eight coloured fish per child. (See illustration, p. 119.) Each fish is a different colour and has one of the virtues from the memory text printed on it: faith, goodness, knowledge, self-control, endurance, godliness, mutual affection, and love. Make sure that each virtue is written on the same coloured fish for each child so that they can identify the virtue by colour if they cannot read.
- Small pieces of magnet attached to each fish at the mouth end, sticking out from the paper
- Small pieces of magnet attached to the end of the string on the straw to make a hook
- Fishing pole, one per child, made from a plastic straw with a string slit through a hole poked at one end (and magnet on the other end of the string)

Note: a small hole in each fish and an unfolded paper clip also works, but children will need more help in catching their fish.

Instructions

a. Introduce the memory passage beginning with . . ."Do your best to add goodness to your faith."
b. Have children fish for each virtue as you say them. Since most of the children cannot read, identify the virtue by colour.
c. When children catch the correct fish with their poles, they may put them into the net and boat made during craft time.

2. Play *Follow the Leader*. "Jesus" is the leader, and children try to follow the action of Jesus. This can include skipping, jumping, hopping, fishing, etc. Allow different children to be "Jesus" whom the others will "follow."

3. Share a snack together. Be sure the children have a rest-room break and wash their hands before snack time.

Gather and Bless

1. Assemble the group for your closing time together.

2. Present the puppet play "An Invitation to Follow." See Early Childhood Resources, page 145, for the play.

3. Begin to learn the Bible memory passage. See pages 143-144 for Bible memory ideas.

3. Review several of the songs you sang during Worship.

4. Dismiss the children with a word of blessing and encouragement.

Jesus said, "Follow me." (Mark 1:17)

121
EARLY CHILDHOOD

Session 2

An Invitation to Faith: From Faith to Failure to Faith

> **Bible Text:** Matthew 14:22-33
> **Story Focus:** Peter's initial faith in Jesus faltered when he attempted to walk on the water to meet Jesus. After Jesus rescued him, Peter and the disciples believed that Jesus was God's special son.
> **Faith Focus:** When we focus on Jesus, we can do more than we think we can.

Gather and Greet

Welcome each child by name. Take attendance and collect any offering. Engage the children in a play activity.

Worship

1. Sing together. Review songs from yesterday. Choose from the following songs found in Early Childhood Resources, pages 156-159. Repeat your theme song to introduce the story.
   "Hallelujah Ballad–Peter"
   "Jesus and His Friends"
   "God's Family"
   "Together"
   "Fisherman Peter" (Worship Resource, page 55)
2. Present the Bible story. This story requires active participation by the children as the story is being told. The instructions in the brackets will be started by the leader, and the children will join in.

Somebody told me that Peter, James, and John are on the shores of Lake Galilee working on their nets. Jesus is there, too. I wonder, would you children like to walk down to the seaside to hear what Jesus is teaching the people today? So many people crowd around Jesus. Maybe we can get close to him.

Let's start walking. [*Walk on the spot.*] Maybe we should walk faster because we may miss some special happenings. [*Run on the spot; then do motions for "crossing the field" by running faster; "going up the hill" by slowing the running and breathing more heavily; "going down the other side of the hill" by running faster.*]

Here we are at the seaside. Let's sit down and watch. [*All sit down.*] Look at all those people. They must have been here all day because the disciples are telling the people to sit down for something to eat. Jesus is helping them feed all those people.

Now Jesus is telling Peter and the other disciples to get into the boat and row to the other side. It is getting dark. Jesus is sending the people home. Then he will go to the hillside to pray to God.

See Peter and his friends rowing in the boat. Can you hear them singing? [*Sing to tune: "Row, Row, Row Your Boat."*]

Peter, Peter, row your boat,
On Lake Galilee.
Jesus said to row your boat,
To the other side.

I wonder what they are talking about now. They were all excited about so many people having enough food to eat. Now they are looking up at the darkening sky. They are listening to that wind. Do you hear it? It is getting stronger and stronger. [*Some make blowing sounds with their hands cupped around the mouth, while others make "wooing" sounds.*] It is so dark now. Peter and his friends can hardly row the boat in the wind. They are getting worried about the bad weather.

All of a sudden they see someone walking toward them on top of the water! Is it a ghost? They become very frightened. But it isn't a ghost. It is Jesus. He says, "Do not be afraid. It is I."

Then Peter stood up. He was all excited to see Jesus. "Lord, if it is really you, let me come walking on the water to you."

Jesus says to Peter, "Yes, come." So, there is Peter climbing out of the boat onto the water. First he hangs on tightly to the side of the boat, but when he sees Jesus standing there, he lets go of the boat, and he, too, is walking on top of the water.

But when Peter looked away from Jesus, he started to fall down, splash, into the water. Now he is afraid again. He shouts to Jesus, "Lord, save me!" Jesus reached out his hand and helped Peter.

Jesus said to Peter, "Why are you afraid?" Together they step into the boat. And no one is afraid any more because Jesus is with them.

When we are afraid because there is a storm, or when we become lost, we can ask Jesus to help us. We can trust Jesus. He loves you and me, just as he loved Peter.

[*Sing to tune: "Row, Row, Row Your Boat."*]
When I'm afraid in a storm,
Jesus says to me,
"Do not be afraid, my child
For I love you so."

3. Pray together. "Dear God, thank you for being with Peter during the storm. Thank you for being with us when we are afraid. Amen."

Respond

1. Reinforce the Bible story. Retell the story several times so that the children have the opportunity to do several of the actions.

Supplies

- Small tub filled with water
- Plastic straws
- Plastic boat from Session 1 Bible story
- Small pieces of play dough (3/4 in., 1.8 cm., pieces)
- Small piece of florist oasis
- Figures of Jesus, Peter, and three more disciples made from Popsicle sticks

Instructions:

To make Popsicle-stick figures, you will need Popsicle sticks with small circles of brown construction paper glued to one end. On these circles, draw the faces of Jesus, Peter, and three disciples. Place the stick figures of the disciples in play dough. Place the stick figure of Jesus in a piece of florist oasis.

Retell the story using the motions from before. When the disciples go into the boat, place the stick figures for disciples and Peter in the boat. To create the storm, have children make waves by blowing into the water through the straws. Some can make the wind sounds. Place the Jesus Popsicle stick in the water.

2. To develop the concept of trust with the children, take a trust walk. First, have everyone join hands and close their eyes. Lead them on a short walk to see if they trust you enough not to peek. If this activity works well, invite them to choose partners. One will close her or his eyes and be led by the other. After a few minutes, exchange positions.

Talk about trust. When do children need to trust God to help them? Invite them to talk about times that they were afraid and trusted Jesus. Even though we cannot see Jesus, he is with us. We can trust that he hears us when we are afraid.

3. Continue making the Accordion Activity Booklet. Add the page for Session 2 (page 126). Distribute the page and crayons. Have the children colour the picture. Place the child's name on the back of the page. Set pages aside.

Make-It

Choose from the following activities:

1. Make a sponge-painted picture.

Supplies

- Paper
- Poster paints: several colours premixed in aluminum pie plates
- Small pieces of sponge
- Paint shirt for each child

Instructions

a. Distribute sponge and paper.
b. Invite the children to draw pictures that remind them that Jesus is with people when they are afraid.
c. Set pictures aside to dry.

2. Make a container for grass. Faith means expecting something to happen even when we cannot see it happening. To illustrate faith for children, make a container and plant grass seed. The children will observe growth.

Supplies

- Bottom of a plastic 2-litre pop bottle (pre-cut)
- One strip (approximately 1 in., 2.5 cm.) of plastic cut from the pop bottle to form a handle.
- Paper fasteners (brads) to attach handle to the container
- Paper punch to make two holes in the side of the container for the handle
- Potting soil, enough to fill each container to 1 inch from the top
- Grass seed

Instructions

a. Distribute the container, a handle, and two fasteners to each child. Attach the handle to the container.

b. Fill containers with potting soil. Add grass seed by sprinkling it on top of the soil and working it in with fingers.

c. Encourage the children to watch daily to see what happens. Thank God together for making things grow.

Games and Snacks

1. Try an obstacle-course relay. This game can help children gain self-confidence in doing things that may seem scary.

Supplies

- Beanbags
- Plastic hoops
- Wood boards (6 in. x 6 ft., 15 cm. x 2.75 m.)
- Towels
- Boxes or stacking crates

Instructions

a. Set up several obstacle courses using the materials: hoop, board, towel, then box.

b. Form lines with an equal number of children in each line. The first child in each line places a beanbag on her or his head. She then steps into the hoop, picks it up over her head, then back down on the ground. Next she walks on the board without stepping off, then steps onto the towel. At the towel, she must take off the beanbag and toss it into the box. She then retrieves the beanbag and delivers it to the next child in the line.

| x | hoop | board | towel | box |

2. Play *Follow the Leader*. "Jesus" is the leader and children try to follow the actions of Jesus. Use the same actions you used in Session 1. Add such actions as "walking on water," "taking your eyes off Jesus and falling," "climbing into the boat."

3. Have a rest-room break. Share a snack.

Gather and Bless

1. Assemble the total group for closing time.

2. Present the puppet play "A Test of Faith." See Early Childhood Resources, page 146, for the play.

3. Review the memory verses. See page 115 for Bible memory ideas.

4. Close with singing.

5. Thank the children for coming and give them a word of blessing as they leave.

I will trust in God and will not be afraid. (Isaiah 12:2)

Permission is granted to photocopy this page.

Session 3

An Invitation to Loyalty: From Loyalty to Betrayal

Bible Texts: John 13:34-38; Mark 14:66-72
Biblical Background: John 13:1-38; John 18:1-11; Luke 22:51; John 19:1—20:1-23
Story Focus: Peter wanted to be a loyal friend to Jesus, but when frightening things that he did not understand began to happen, he denied the friendship. Even though Peter did not pass the loyalty test, Jesus continued to love him.
Faith Focus: It is easy to slip back into old patterns of behaviour when we are faced with new and frightening situations. Jesus continues to love and forgive us even when we do not act like his friend.

Gather and Greet

Welcome each child by name. Encourage them to participate in an activity. Take attendance and collect the offering.

Worship

1. Sing together. Use songs from Early Childhood Resources, pages 156-159.
"Together"
"Hallelujah Ballad–Peter"
"Praise the Lord"
"Fisherman Peter" (Worship Resource, page 55)
"Jesus Listens When I Pray"
2. Present the Bible story. Remember that your tone of voice and facial expressions can convey much of the emotion of the story.

Peter and Jesus had become very good friends. Peter said that he wanted to go with Jesus wherever he went.

Peter said, "I'm his friend; I'm his friend."

But Jesus knew that there soon would be times when Peter would try to forget all about Jesus. Jesus told Peter, "Before the rooster crows two times, you will tell people that you do not know me!"

One night Jesus was out with his friends when some soldiers came to find him. They did not like some of the things Jesus said or did because he was teaching new things about God. When Peter found out that they wanted to take Jesus away, he took out his sword and cut off the ear of one of the soldiers. As he did this he thought to himself, "I'm his friend; I'm his friend."

But Jesus told Peter that he should not have hurt the soldier. Jesus touched the soldier and healed his ear. The soldiers arrested Jesus and took him away to the rulers.

Peter followed along behind when the soldiers took Jesus away. At one place, a girl was standing at the door. She said to Peter, "You are one of Jesus' friends, aren't you?"

Peter became frightened and said, "No, I'm not his friend, not his friend!" A little while later, another person asked Peter, "You are one of Jesus' friends, aren't you?"

Again Peter replied, "No, I'm not his friend, not his friend." And once more, someone else asked Peter, "Were you not just with your friend Jesus?"

One more time Peter said, "I AM NOT HIS FRIEND!"

Suddenly the rooster crowed. Peter remembered what Jesus had said about the rooster crowing. Peter was sorry that he had said Jesus was not his friend. Peter started to cry because he really liked Jesus very much and wanted to be his friend.

Peter was sad about the way he treated Jesus. Deep down in his heart, he knew that Jesus still loved him very, very much and was still his friend.

3. Pray together. "Dear God, thank you that Jesus still wanted to be friends with Peter. Thank you that you will always be my friend, too. Amen."

Respond

1. Retell the story with the children's help, using actions at appropriate times. Begin the story with everyone holding hands in a circle. When you come to "I'm his friend," shake hands up and down. When you come to "I'm not his friend," let go of hands and shake heads from side to side. Join hands again until the next time.

2. Talk about the story. Help the children think about the following questions:
- Why do you think Peter was afraid to be Jesus' friend?
- How did Peter show that he was sorry for the things he said about his friend Jesus?
  Talk about friends:
- Who are your friends?
- What do you do with your friends?
- What happens when you do or say something that hurts your friend?
- How do you show that you are sorry?
  Jesus wants to be our friend.
- How can we show Jesus that we want to be his friend, too?
  When we say unkind things or hurt our friends, this makes Jesus sad.
- How can we show Jesus that we are sorry for what we have done?
  Jesus loves us and wants to keep being our friend even when we make him

sad. Jesus will forgive us, just as he forgave Peter. Jesus will keep on being our friend.

3. Continue making the Accordion Activity Booklet. Use page 132 for Session 3. Let the children colour the pictures. Print the child's name on the picture. Set pictures aside.

Make-It

Choose one of the following activities:

1. Make friendship beads. See illustration. Children are encouraged to make something to give to friends to show that their friendship is appreciated. Suggest that the children give their gifts to someone who is not attending these sessions.

Supplies

- Triangles of coloured construction paper, four or five for each child
- 28 in., 70 cm. yarn, string or shoelace
- White glue in small containers
- Cotton swabs
- Straw or pencil for rolling

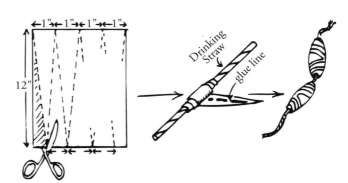

Instructions

a. Precut triangles from construction paper, each measuring 1 x 12 in., 2.5 x 30 cm.
b. Distribute five triangles, a straw or pencil, glue, and a cotton swab to each child.
c. Place a dab of glue down the centre of the triangle. Wrap the triangle around the straw, starting at the smaller end. Continue rolling, centring the point if possible.
d. Spread extra glue to coat the outside of the rolled bead. Slide it off the straw and stand it on its end to dry.
e. Thread yarn through the dry beads. Tie ends to form a necklace.

Note: If you have enough time, make one for each child to keep. Three or four beads are enough for each necklace. Encourage the children to make more friendship beads at home.

2. Make friendship cards.

Supplies

- Construction paper
- Copies of the page with "You are my friend" (page 131) written in bubble letters
- Crayons
- Stickers, glitter, etc.

Instructions

a. Children colour and decorate the paper given or design their own cards.
b. An adult prints the name of the friend to whom the card will be given.

3. Make friendship cookies. Bake and decorate cookies, one for each child and one to give away to a friend.

Games and Snacks

1. Play *Tap, Tap, Hug*. This game is similar to the familiar *Duck, Duck, Goose*. Instead of chasing each other, try holding hands and walking or hopping around the circle. As the game continues, the person hugged should hug someone who has not been hugged before until all have had a turn.

2. Play *May I?* The group stands in a circle around Jesus (adult). "Jesus" calls out good choices or not-so-good choices of action and/or behaviour. Examples are: help to set the table, pick up toys, make my bed, hold an adult's hand when crossing the street, hit a friend when he takes my toy, shouts at mom when she turns off the television. The whole group must decide if it is a good choice or not. If it is a good choice, everyone takes a step toward the centre. If it is a "not-so-good" choice, the group does not move forward. When the group meets in the centre, everyone participates in a group hug. Comment that Peter made a few choices that were not so good, but Jesus continued to be his friend.

3. Play *Follow the Leader*. Start in a circle, holding hands. The leader twists and turns so that it is difficult for the children to keep on holding hands. Assure the children that if they let go, it is all right. They should join hands and try again. Although Peter disappointed his friend Jesus, he could try again. Jesus would still be his friend.

4. Share a snack after the children have a rest-room break.

Gather and Bless

1. Assemble the group for closing time.
2. Present the puppet play "A Test of Loyality." See page 147 for the play.
3. Review the memory verses. See page 115 for Bible memory ideas.
4. Sing several songs.
5. Give each child a word of blessing as you dismiss them.

You Are My Friends

Permission is granted to photocopy this page.

Session 3

As I have loved you, love one another. (John 13:34)

Permission is granted to photocopy this page.

An Invitation to Courage: From Fear to Courage

Bible Text: Acts 2:1-42

Story Focus: At Pentecost, God's Spirit changed Peter from a fearful follower to a courageous leader. Peter was no longer afraid to tell others about Jesus when he realized that the Holy Spirit was helping him.

Faith Focus: When we let God's Holy Spirit live in us, we are given courage to act boldly for Jesus.

Worship

1. Sing together. Choose from the following songs found in Early Childhood Resources, pages 156-159.

"Hallelujah Ballad–Peter"

"God's Family"

"Jesus Listens When I Pray"

"Praise the Lord"

"Jesus and His Friends"

2. Present the Bible story. Peter tells this story. An adult, in the role of the Holy Spirit, wears a light-coloured cape and carries coloured streamers (2 ft., 60 cm., in length) to place on the heads of the children at the appropriate time. The children are part of the believers in the story.

After I had told everyone that Jesus was not my friend, I felt very sad. But when Jesus looked at me, I knew that he forgave me, and that he still loved me very much. Now Jesus had gone back to heaven. He gave us a special message before he left. He said, "You must wait in the city until God's power comes down upon you."

We were waiting for Jesus to send us God's special power. It was a special day called Pentecost. People from many countries gathered to worship God. But we were afraid. Some people did not like it that we still followed Jesus.

Suddenly, while we were waiting and praying, we heard a sound like a very strong wind.

Can we make the sound of a strong wind? Let's try. . . . [*Make wind sounds together. While the wind blows, the Holy Spirit enters and places a streamer on the head or shoulder of each child and adult.*]

Then another strange thing happened. There were flames of fire that were not burning anything. These flames rested on the heads of the people there. As these flames rested on us, another strange thing happened. Everybody started to talk at once, and in different languages. Strangers could understand what we were saying in their very own language! We were so excited. We started to tell everyone about our friend, Jesus, and the power that God gave to us. Because they could understand what we were saying, others became excited. All of us started cheering and praising God for this new, wonderful power God had given us. This was the power of the Holy Spirit that Jesus had promised!

You know, girls and boys, I became a changed person after this. No longer could I remain quiet. I wanted everyone to know about Jesus, how he taught us, how he died and then came alive again, how he lives with God now in heaven.

Everyone who knew me before saw that I had changed. I was not afraid anymore. I believed what Jesus said because the Holy Spirit that he had promised to help us was with us now. I am a changed person, and I am very happy.

3. Pray together. "Dear God, thank you for changing me and giving me courage to talk to others about you. Thank you for sending a helper to show me how to live. Amen."

Respond

1. Review the story using the following echo pantomime. The leader says the phrase slowly and does the motions. Then the children repeat the phrase and mime the actions of the leader. Begin by having everyone stand in a circle. Encourage the children to say and do exactly what the leader does.

When the day of Pentecost came [*Do a morning stretch with arms in air*]
we were all together in one place [*Sit on the floor*].
We were afraid, so we sat quietly [*Hold finger to mouth saying, "Shhhh"*].
Suddenly [*Look startled*],
there came a sound from heaven [*Cock your head to one side as if listening for an airplane*],
the sound of a strong wind [*Blow hard*]
that filled the house where we were sitting [*Hold hands to cover ears*].
Flames like fire rested on each person [*Point and look in awe at another's head*].
Everyone was filled with the Holy Spirit [*Start with hands at side and move up body to reach into the air*]
and began to speak in other languages [*Louez a Dieu, Amigos de Cristo*].
The people were amazed [*Register surprise as you cup hand to ear*],
because they understood about God [*Change surprise to joy—smile*].
But Peter stood up and said [*Stand up*],
"Listen to what I say [*Raise hand and point finger for attention*].
God sent Jesus to show us how to live [*Point upwards then sweep over the group on "us"*].

Believe in Jesus and be baptized" [*Fold hands and bow head*].
Many people believed and were baptized [*Fold hands and bow head again*].
And everybody praised God [*Join hands and skip to the left as a group*].
Amen [*Sit on floor*].

2. Talk about the story. Encourage the children to think about these questions:
- How did Peter know Jesus still loved him?
- How would you have felt if you had been in the room that day?
- The Holy Spirit helped Peter to be brave. When do we need help to be brave?
- How can the Holy Spirit help us say the right words?
- How can we show we love God?

3. Continue assembling the Accordion Activity Booklet. Distribute crayons and page 137 for Session 4. Have the children colour the picture. Write their names on the pictures. You will need to assemble the booklet before Session 5. See page 114 for instructions. On day five, the children will colour a picture, glue it onto this final page, and take their booklets home.

Make-It

Choose one of the following craft activities to help the children remember today's Bible story. You may wish to offer both options and let each child choose one craft to make.

1. Make a pinwheel. See illustration. A pinwheel can remind the children of this special event in Peter's life, assuring them that God's Spirit gives courage. Wind is a symbol of God's power and the Holy Spirit.

Supplies

- Squares (6 in., 15 cm.) of coloured construction paper
- Crayons or markers
- Scissors
- Straight pins or small nails
- 1/4 in., .62 cm., dowels (12 in., 30 cm., in length) or plastic straws

Instructions

  a. Cut with scissors toward the centre (see diagram).
  b. Bring each corner to the centre.
  c. Fasten to the straw or dowel with the pin or nail. The pinwheel should spin easily on the dowel.

2. Make lunch-bag puppets.

Supplies

- Lunch bags that have a folded bottom
- Pieces of felt, fabric, buttons, plastic eyes, yarn, etc.
- Glue
- Yellow adhesive or construction paper for "tongues of fire"

Instructions

  a. Distribute one lunch bag per person.
  b. Using cloth scraps, etc., make a face on the bottom of the bag while it remains folded. The mouth becomes the bottom edge of the fold.

c. When the puppets are completed, help them say, "We will tell about what we saw and heard."

d. Give children the opportunity to retell the story of Pentecost to each other.

Games and Snacks

1. Play *Follow the Leader*. Distribute the streamers used in the Bible story. Have children follow the leader in creative movement with the streamers. Some suggestions: balance the streamer on your head and sway back and forth; throw it into the air and try to catch it without using your hands; form a long caterpillar line by hanging loosely onto a streamer in front and behind, then let go and jump up and down in butterfly fashion. Use this activity as a reminder of the change in Peter's life when he became filled with the Holy Spirit.

2. Play *Spread the Spirit Tag*. Assign one person to be It. It has a streamer tied on It's forehead. When It tags a child, It ties a streamer around that child's forehead, who then becomes an additional It. The game continues until all are caught by the Spirit and are wearing a streamer. The last one caught becomes the new It.

Gather and Bless

1. Gather together.

2. Present the puppet play "A Test of Courage." See Early Childhood Resources, page 149, for the play.

3. Review the memory verses. See page 115 for Bible memory ideas.

4. Sing several favourite songs.

5. Dismiss the children with a smile and words of encouragement.

Session 4

You will receive the gift of the Holy Spirit.

(Acts 2:38b)

Permission is granted to photocopy this page.

Session 5

An Invitation to Acceptance: From Rejection to Acceptance

Bible Text: Acts 10:1-48
Story Focus: After a vision from God, Peter believed that it was not right for him to be prejudiced against people who were not Jews. All people are equally accepted by God.
Faith Focus: When we think like God, we value all people as God does.

Worship

1. Sing together. Sing your theme song. Let the children choose their favourites. Spend extra time enjoying singing praise to God. See Early Childhood Resources, pages 156-159, for a complete listing of songs.

2. Present the Bible story. Tell the story the first time without the props mentioned in the parentheses. Make the minor adjustments necessary for use without props.

This is Peter's house. [*Tape Peter onto the box.*] Peter loved God. [*Add heart with cross inside.*] One day Peter had a dream. [*Add cloud.*] In the dream, God was talking to Peter. God showed Peter lots of things to eat. Some of the things were foods that Peter was not supposed to eat. But God told Peter it was okay to eat those things. He told him to go and visit a man named Cornelius.

This is Cornelius's house. [*Add Cornelius to the other box.*] Cornelius loved God, too. [*Add heart with cross.*] Cornelius had a dream, too [*Add cloud.*], and someone talked to him. He was told to invite Peter to his house. He and Peter did not know each other. They were not even friends yet. But Cornelius invited Peter to his house anyway.

When Peter arrived at Cornelius's house [*Move Peter to second box.*], there were lots of people there. [*Add crowd.*]

Cornelius said, "We are glad you have come. Please tell us about God."

Peter said, "At first I did not think I should come, because we do not even know each other. But God told me that I could come to your house and even eat the food you have that is different from the food I am supposed to eat. God says that we should be friends. God wants me to tell you about a special friend, Jesus. Jesus and I were friends for a long time. Then Jesus died, and we couldn't see him anymore. But Jesus is still with us as a very special friend. God gave us the Holy Spirit to be that friend and help us understand what God wants us to do.

After Peter told about Jesus and the Holy Spirit, Cornelius and his friends wanted to have the Holy Spirit for a special friend, too.

Peter told them that the Holy Spirit comes to people in ways people don't always understand–sometimes like a cloud [*Place cloud on box.*], sometimes like a flame [*flame*], sometimes in different languages [*Place letters in no set order.*], sometimes as a person [*brightly dressed*], and sometimes like the wind.

Peter said, "We are different in many ways. We may eat different kinds of food, we live in different places, we look differently, and we talk differently. But God loves each one of us and wants us to be God's friends. God and Jesus and the Holy Spirit help us to be friends."

Peter and Cornelius hugged each other and prayed together. [*Put puppets close together.*]

3. Pray together. "God, thank you that Peter could tell Cornelius about you. Thank you that we can learn about you, too. I love you, God. Thank you that Jesus and the Holy Spirit can be our best friends. Help us to tell our friends about you. Amen."

Respond

1. Retell the story. Be sure all the children have a chance to participate.

Supplies

- Two large cardboard boxes to place symbols onto and to play inside later
- Paper symbols/pictures: hearts with cross inside, cloud, foods, animals, pictures of people for a crowd, flame, several letters of the alphabet, picture for Holy Spirit, puppets of Peter and Cornelius
- Crayons
- Glue or tape

Instructions

Before retelling the story, have each child colour a symbol. At the appropriate times in the story, glue or tape the symbols to the boxes.

2. Spend time talking about the story. Encourage the children to take turns responding.

- How are we different from each other? (looks, size, preferences about colours, toys, food, television shows)
- How do we treat people who look and sound different from us?
- Does God like people with brown eyes better than people with blue eyes?

God loves each person just the way we are. God wants to be our friend. God wants us to be friends with other children even if they are different from us.

3. Finish the last page of the Accordion Activity Booklet. Distribute crayons and page 142 for Session 5. Have the children complete and colour

the picture. Attach this final page to the activity booklet. Take the time to review the booklet as a reminder of the Bible stories for the week.

Make-It

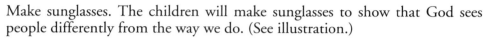

Make sunglasses. The children will make sunglasses to show that God sees people differently from the way we do. (See illustration.)

Supplies
- Cardboard from cereal boxes
- Scissors, tape
- Plastic cut from green pop bottles
- Elastic or string

Instructions
a. Cut a cardboard pattern to fit a child's head. (See illustration.)
b. Cut pieces of green plastic to fit inside the eye holes.
c. Slide the plastic into place and tape securely.
d. Fit on child's head with elastic or string.
e. Allow time for the children to look at each other and objects of nature through these different glasses. Use the sunglasses for the game *Guess Whom God Loves?*

Games and Snacks

1. Make popcorn together. Have a supply of different toppings such as a mixture of sugar and cinnamon, seasoned salt, spices, or garlic. Tell the children that God made each of us with different tastes and likes. It is all right that one likes sweet popcorn and one likes salty popcorn.

2. Play *Guess Whom God Loves?* The leader helps the children chant the rhyme. Then the leader gives a clue and all try to guess who is being chosen. Repeat the rhyming activity until each person has been chosen.

Rhyme
All: A,B,C, let me see [*Make hands into glasses and look around, or use the sunglasses from the craft time.*]
Teacher: God loves someone who is . . . [*wearing a pink bow, green shoes, is lying down*].
Teacher: God loves _____[*name of child*], and God loves me.
All: God loves _____[*repeat name*], and God loves me.

3. Play *Follow the Leader.* Try some of these variations.
a. Sit in a circle. The leader does the action, and the children copy in turn around the circle.
b. Each person does a silly action and then looks across the circle and tries to copy someone else. If everyone cooperates, all might be doing the same thing after a while.
Note: This can be funny, but can also show that people watch what we are doing and can learn from us just as Cornelius learned from Peter.

4. Play some cultural games. Check the games on pages 94-96. Adapt the games to fit your children.

Gather and Bless

1. Assemble the group for closing time.

2. Present the puppet play "A Test of Acceptance." See Early Childhood Resources, page 150, for the play.

3. Review the memory verses. See page 115 for ideas.

4. Sing your theme song.

5. Thank each child for being part of your class. Give each one a word of blessing.

God treats all people alike. (Acts 10:34b)

Permission is granted to photocopy this page.

Resources

Bible memory

2 Peter 1:3, 5-7

Ideas for learning the passage each session

Session 1: Children will begin to learn the list of virtues in their "fishing" game. See pages 119-120.

Session 2: Print the words on construction paper or felt boats, using the same colour scheme as in Session 1. Cut each boat into three or four puzzle pieces. Create a seascape picture on a large piece of flannel graph or bristol board. Distribute the puzzle pieces to the children, have them assemble the boats and repeat the words as they are attached to the picture. Repeat this activity several times.

Session 3: Make a puzzle in the shape of a cross using the memory words.

Session 4: Write words on coloured "flames" and attach to a streamer.

Session 5: Use butterfly shapes and fasten to a white sheet.

Note: If you use the same colour for each virtue each day, the children who cannot read will be able to recognize the words by their colour.

Other ideas

1. Use echo effect memorization. You will need tin cans, with both ends removed, for half of the number of children present. One-half of the group will say the first phrase. Then the second half repeats the words through the tin cans, creating an echo effect. Exchange groups and repeat.

2. Try a clothesline memory game. Form groups of eight children. Give each child one word from the memory "virtues," using the same colour code and light cardboard or construction paper as used previously. Set up "clotheslines" by having two people hold a piece of rope between them or by tying the ends of the rope to two chairs. Set out sixteen clothespins for each group. See how long it takes for each group to "hang up" the memory words in the correct order. Encourage competition against the clock rather than another group.

3. If you feel that this memory text provided is too difficult, use these short Scripture verses for each day.

Session 1: Jesus said, "Follow me, and I will make you fish for people." (NRSV) Mark 1:17

Session 2: I will trust [in God], and will not be afraid. (NRSV) Isaiah 12:2

Session 3: Just as I have loved you, you also should love one another.

(NRSV) John 13:34

    Session 4: . . . you will receive the gift of the Holy Spirit. (NRSV) Acts 2:38b

    Session 5: . . . it is true that God treats all people alike. (NRSV) Acts 10:34b

Puppet plays

Session 1

"An Invitation to Follow"

Cast: Bumble Bear, Rocky Raccoon, Hooty Owl, Honey Bunny, and Dog
Setting: *The play begins with Honey Bunny being chased by Dog. Suddenly Rocky Raccoon appears and pushes Honey Bunny off the stage. The dog looks around the stage, sniffing. When he cannot find Honey Bunny, Dog leaves the stage. Honey Bunny comes on stage with Bumble Bear, Rocky Raccoon, and Hooty Owl.*

Honey Bunny:	Thank you for saving me from the farmer's dog. My name is Honey Bunny.
Bumble Bear:	Hi! It is nice to meet you, Honey Bunny. My name is Bumble Bear.
Hooty Owl:	My name is Hooty Owl, Hooty Owl.
Rocky Raccoon:	And my name is Rocky Raccoon. Why was the farmer's dog chasing you?
Honey Bunny:	Because I ran away.
Hooty Owl:	Away from where, away from where?
Honey Bunny:	From my home. You see, when I was a baby bunny, the farmer caught me in his garden. He put me into a little house with a wire fence all around it. But I escaped.
Hooty Owl:	Why did you escape? Why?
Honey Bunny:	Because every day I would look through the fence and wonder what it would be like to live out in the woods again, like I did when I was a baby. Today I dug a hole under the fence and escaped.
Rocky Raccoon:	Good for you! I think it would be awful to be kept shut in a little pen all day.
Honey Bunny:	Oh, it is not so bad. The farmer is kind to me and gives me lots of lettuce and carrots to eat.
Bumble Bear:	Still you are a wild animal and should be free. Would you like to live here in the woods with us?
Hooty Owl:	Oh yes, do, do!
Honey Bunny:	Thank you, but I should be going home now. The farmer will be looking for me.
Rocky Raccoon:	Oh, please stay with us. We could be your friends.
Honey Bunny:	It would be nice to have friends, but I must go back.
Hooty Owl:	But why? Why?
Honey Bunny:	Well, because I am afraid.

Bumble Bear:	Afraid of what?
Honey Bunny:	I am afraid to live out here in the woods. At home I am kept safe in my little house, and the farmer feeds me every day.
Rocky Raccoon:	But if you lived with us you would have friends, and we would take care of you.
Bumble Bear:	Yes, and every day would be an adventure!
Rocky Raccoon:	I know it can be scary to move to a new home. Sometimes we are afraid to try new things and go to new places, but we have a special friend called Jesus. Jesus is always with us wherever we go. We are never alone. Jesus loves us very much, and he teaches us to love and help one another when we are afraid.
Honey Bunny:	It is good to have friends and to know that we are not alone. Yes, I will stay here with you. This will be my new home, and we will go on many happy adventures together. [*All the puppets are happy. They hug and kiss Honey Bunny.*]
Bumble Bear:	Come on, let's show Honey Bunny her new home. [*The puppets are laughing and dancing as they go off the stage.*]

Session 2

"A Test of Faith"

Cast: Bumble Bear, Rocky Raccoon, Hooty Owl and Honey Bunny
Props: A rolled cardboard tube with a slit along one side. The tube is fastened securely to the puppet stage along its side. The puppets appear to enter one end of the tube and disappear inside (see illustration).
Setting: *The play begins with all the puppets on stage.*

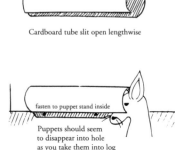

Cardboard tube slit open lengthwise

fasten to puppet stand inside

Puppets should seem to disappear into hole as you take them into log

Rocky Raccoon:	Oh look! A log! Maybe there is some food inside.
Bumble Bear:	[*Smelling the air*] Hmmm, it smells like honey!
Hooty Owl:	I wonder if there are any buzzing bees around, buzzing bees around?
Rocky Raccoon:	I will go inside first to make sure it is safe. [*Rocky goes inside the hole and quickly returns.*] Yes it is safe. There are no bees inside but there is plenty of honey! [*Rocky returns into the log and the sound of smacking lips is heard.*]
Honey Bunny:	Oh, do hurry, Rocky. I am so hungry! [*Rocky Raccoon comes out of the hole and Honey Bunny goes inside.*]
Honey Bunny:	Going into holes is easy for me! [*With Honey Bunny inside the log the sound of smacking lips is heard.*]
Hooty Owl:	It sounds very delicious, very delicious! [*Honey Bunny comes out of the hole and Hooty Owl goes inside. The sound of smacking lips is heard once again.*]
Hooty Owl:	[*Comes out of hole*] It is your turn, Bumble Bear, your turn. [*Bumble Bear tries to go into the hole headfirst but is too*

large; he tries to go in by his rear, the other puppets try to push, but he is just too large.]

Bumble Bear: Oh dear, I shall go hungry because I am too large to fit into that tiny hole. I wish I could have some honey. It is my favourite food. [*Bumble Bear cries.*]

Honey Bunny: Surely we can think of a way to help Bumble Bear get inside the log to get some honey.

Hooty Owl: I know, I know, just have faith, have faith.

Rocky Raccoon: That's right. We must believe there is a way. Hey, maybe your whole body is too big, but maybe just your paw would fit inside the hole.

Bumble Bear: No, it won't work. I'm too large. I won't get any honey. [*He cries.*]

Rocky Raccoon: You must have faith, Bumble Bear. God would not have given bears the desire to eat honey if there was no way to get it.
[*Grumbling, Bumble Bear tries to put his paw into the hole. It fits. He pulls it out and puts it to his mouth.*]

Honey Bunny: See, Bumble, sometimes when we think we can't do something, we just have to have faith.

Hooty Owl: Yea! Faith is believing, faith is believing.

Rocky Raccoon: If we think we cannot do something, it is good to have friends to help and encourage us. So, if we are afraid to try new things, we can ask our special friend, Jesus, to help us. When we remember that Jesus is always with us, we can try to do things we thought were too hard.

Bumble Bear: Thank you, my good friends, for helping me to believe that I could have some honey from the log. It was good!

Hooty Owl: Now that we have eaten, let us go and play, go and play. [*The puppets go off the stage laughing and chasing one another.*]

Session 3

"A Test of Loyalty"

Cast: Bumble Bear, Rocky Raccoon, Hooty Owl, and Honey Bunny
Props: Large cardboard tree securely fastened to one side of the puppet stage, four small plastic or cardboard eggs, sound of thunder (can be made with your voice or by shaking a thin sheet of metal or tin), lightning (get a helper to turn the lights on and off quickly occasionally throughout the play, in unison with the thunder)
Setting: *Bumble Bear, Rocky Raccoon, Hooty Owl, and Honey Bunny are huddled under the large tree. There is a terrible storm with the sound of thunder and flashes of lightning.*

Honey Bunny: I wish this storm would stop. This tree is not a safe place to hide. I am so afraid.

Hooty Owl: Me, too! Me, too!

Bumble Bear: Well, I wish the storm would stop, too, because I'm hungry! We cannot go out in this storm to look for food.

Rocky Raccoon: Yes, I'm hungry, too. Before I met you, I would steal my food from the farmer.

Honey Bunny:	Stealing is wrong, Rocky. Jesus does not want anyone to steal. I am very hungry, too. I am so hungry that I have a tummy ache.
Hooty Owl:	Me, too! Me, too! [*There is more thunder and lightning. The puppets huddle closer together except for Rocky Raccoon who slips off the stage.*]
Honey Bunny:	[*Hugging Bumble Bear*] I do wish this storm would stop!
Hooty Owl:	[*Looking around*] Hey, where is Rocky? Where is Rocky!
Bumble Bear:	Oh no, maybe he was hit by lightning. Let's look for him. Maybe he is hurt! [*The puppets spread out to look for Rocky. They look all around the stage calling his name but cannot find him. They go back to huddle under the tree.*]
Bumble Bear:	Oh, dear! We cannot find our friend, Rocky Raccoon. Where can he be?
Hooty Owl:	Maybe we will never see him again, never again. [*Suddenly Rocky appears on stage with four eggs.*]
Rocky Raccoon:	Hi everyone!
Bumble Bear:	[*Angrily*] Where did you go, Rocky? We looked everywhere for you.
Rocky Raccoon:	I brought us some food – four eggs. See, one for each of us.
Hooty Owl:	Where did you get eggs, Rocky? Where?
Rocky Raccoon:	I just found them.
Honey Bunny:	Found them? I think you found them in the farmer's henhouse. Oh, Rocky. How could you? Did you steal those eggs?
Rocky Raccoon:	Well, um, um, gulp.
Honey Bunny:	You did steal them, didn't you? Rocky, you know that it is wrong to steal. Why did you do it?
Rocky Raccoon:	Because the storm is so frightening, and we could not all go out to look for food. We were so hungry.
Honey Bunny:	Even though we are hungry and afraid, it is wrong to steal. [*The storm stops.*]
Bumble Bear:	Look! The storm has stopped. Now we can all go out to look for food. We will be safe now. Jesus loves us and takes care of us.
Hooty Owl:	Not Rocky, Jesus doesn't love Rocky. He is bad, he is bad.
Rocky Raccoon:	You're right. Jesus doesn't love me because I did a bad thing when I stole the eggs.
Honey Bunny:	Oh Rocky, Jesus does love you. Jesus does not like us to do bad things, but he still loves us. Hey, I have an idea. Now that the storm has stopped, why don't we help Rocky return the eggs to the henhouse? Then we can go and get some food.
All:	Let's go.
Rocky Raccoon:	Thank you, Jesus, for loving me even when I do bad things. Thank you for being my friend. [*Puppets follow Rocky off the stage.*]

Session 4

"A Test of Courage"

Cast: Bumble Bear, Rocky Raccoon, Hooty Owl, Honey Bunny, and Dog
Setting: *The play begins with the sound of snoring off stage. On stage comes Honey Bunny, looking around.*

Honey Bunny:	Shhh, the others are still sleeping. I am so hungry that I could not sleep. I think I'll look for a snack. [*She begins to look for food. Then she stops and looks up.*] Oh no! I hear the farmer's dog. [*Sound of barking in background. The dog comes on stage, sees Honey Bunny, and begins to chase her around the stage.*]
Honey Bunny:	Help! Help! Please! Someone help me!
Rocky Raccoon:	[*Comes on stage yawning*] What's going on? Who is making all that noise? [*Sees dog chasing Honey Bunny.*]
Honey Bunny:	Help! Help me, Rocky. The farmer's dog is after me. Help! Help!
Rocky Raccoon:	[*Shaking*] Oh no! The dog is chasing Honey Bunny. I should help her, but I'm afraid.
Honey Bunny:	Help me! Help me!
Rocky Raccoon:	I wish I could, but I'm too afraid! [*Rocky goes off stage.*] [*The dog continues to chase Honey Bunny.*]
Honey Bunny:	Help me! Oh please, someone help me!
Hooty Owl:	[*Comes on stage*] Who is yelling for help? Who is yelling for help? [*Hooty Owl sees the dog chasing Honey Bunny.*] Oh dear, oh dear. The farmer's dog is chasing Honey Bunny. I would like to help her but he might catch me. I better fly away. [*Hooty Owl goes up and then disappears into the stage.*] [*The dog continues to chase Honey Bunny.*]
Honey Bunny:	Please, help me! Someone, help me!
Bumble Bear:	[*Comes on stage, stretching, and yawning*] Who woke me up? [*He hears Honey Bunny calling for help.*]
Honey Bunny:	Bumble bear, help me. The farmer's dog is chasing me. [*The dog finally catches Honey Bunny.*]
Honey Bunny:	[*Crying*] Please! Help me!
Bumble Bear:	Oh my goodness, it's the farmer's dog, and he has caught my friend, Honey Bunny. He might catch me next. What should I do?
Honey Bunny:	Bumble, please save me!
Bumble Bear:	I can't help you, Honey Bunny. I'm too afraid! No, wait! I am a bear. God made bears big and strong. Dear God, give me the courage to help my friend. [*Bumble Bear runs over to where the dog is holding Honey Bunny. The dog sees him and lets go of Honey Bunny. He turns and bites Bumble. Bumble and the dog fight. Suddenly Bumble lets out a big roar. The dog is afraid and runs away.*]
Honey Bunny:	[*Hugs and kisses Bumble*) Oh Bumble, you saved me from the farmer's dog.
All:	[*The other animals all gather around Bumble Bear.*]
Rocky Raccoon:	Are you okay, Honey Bunny? I am sorry I was too afraid

	to help you.
Hooty Owl:	Me, too! Me, too! I'm sorry, too.
Rocky and Hooty:	[Together] Oh Bumble, you were so brave.
Bumble Bear:	I was afraid at first, but Jesus gave me the courage to stand up to the farmer's dog. I am glad Jesus gives us courage when we need it.
Honey Bunny:	Oh so am I, so am I!
	[*The puppets all laugh and hug one another as they go off stage.*]

Session 5

"A Test of Acceptance"

Cast: Bumble Bear, Rocky Raccoon, Hooty Owl, and Honey Bunny
Props: Large cardboard tree fastened securely to the puppet stage on one side.
Setting: *Puppets enter, laughing and talking among themselves.*

Bumble Bear:	I'm glad we are friends, even though we are not the same.
Rocky Raccoon:	Yes, I'm happy we are all friends, even though we are different.
Hooty Owl:	Me, too! Me, too! It's nice to be able to play together, even though we do not look alike! Look alike!
Honey Bunny:	What do you mean? We are not the same. What do you mean? We are different. What do you mean? We do not look alike.
Bumble Bear:	Ha-ha. Honey Bunny, just look at me. I am big and strong!
Rocky Raccoon:	Yes, and I'm fat and fuzzy! Hee-hee.
Hooty Owl:	And look at me! Look at me! I have feathers and wings!
Honey Bunny:	Ha-ha. I'm soft and cute. I guess you are right. We are not all the same. We are different. We do not look alike.
Hooty Owl:	I am glad we are such good friends, but there are lots of creatures out there who might want to harm us. I think we should choose a leader. Someone to protect us, someone to protect us.
Honey Bunny:	That would be a good idea. Whom should we choose?
Bumble Bear:	Well, I think I should be the leader.
Rocky Raccoon:	Why should you be the leader?
Bumble Bear:	Because I'm the biggest and the strongest. I'm bigger and stronger than any of you. I can protect you if there is danger nearby. I think I should be the leader.
Rocky Raccoon:	No way! You may be bigger and stronger than the rest of us, Bumble Bear, but I'm the smartest! I know where to get food when we are hungry and where to hide if we are afraid. I think I should be the leader.
Hooty Owl:	Not so! Not so! It should be me. It should be me! I may not be as strong as Bumble Bear or as smart as Rocky Raccoon, but I can see farther and fly higher than any of you! I can see danger coming and warn you. I think I should be the leader.

Honey Bunny:	Hey, what about me? I may not be as strong as Bumble Bear or as smart as Rocky Raccoon or maybe I cannot see as far or fly as high as Hooty Owl, but my long ears can hear danger coming from far away, even when the rest of you are sleeping. I think I should be the leader. [*All start grumbling and fighting.*]
Bumble Bear:	We are not the same. God made bears strong. I can protect myself. I don't need any of you. If I cannot be the leader, then I will go by myself. [*Bumble goes off to a corner of the stage and stands quietly.*]
Rocky Raccoon:	I told you we were different. God made raccoons smart, and I can take care of myself, too. I don't need any of you. [*Rocky goes to the other side of the stage and stands quietly.*]
Hooty Owl:	God made me, too. God made me, too! My eyes will keep me from danger. [*Hooty goes to stand by himself.*]
Honey Bunny:	Well, I don't need any of you either. These long ears that God gave to bunnies will protect me. I'm glad I don't look like any of you. [*Stays where she is, standing quietly.*] [*Suddenly Honey Bunny stands up high like she is listening to something.*] Oh no! I hear the farmer's dog barking. DANGER, DANGER! The farmer's dog is coming. Oh, where will I hide?
Hooty Owl:	I can see him. I can see him. DANGER, DANGER! [*Sound of dog barking.*]
Rocky Raccoon:	Hey! Everyone! I see a place where we can hide. Come on. [*All run under the tree*].
Bumble Bear:	I will stand out here beside the tree and protect you if the dog comes closer. [*Sound of barking fades away.*]
Bumble Bear:	I think the dog is gone.
Rocky Raccoon:	I'm sorry, my friends. If it weren't for you, the dog may have caught me.
Honey Bunny:	I'm sorry, too. I'm glad we have each other. I didn't know where to hide.
Hooty Owl:	I'm sorry, too, sorry, too. My eyes can only see danger coming from far away when I am flying. I need all of you to protect me.
Bumble Bear:	I may be strong, but I had no idea the dog was coming. How could I ever have gotten away without your help?
Honey Bunny:	God made us all special. God gave each one special gifts so we are all important. We all need each other. We are all equal before God. [*The puppets go off stage hugging and complimenting one another on their special gifts.*]

Instructions for making puppets

For the puppet plays you will need five animal puppets: Bumble Bear, Rocky Raccoon, Hooty Owl, Honey Bunny, and Dog.

Supplies
- A large cardboard tree
- A cardboard roll, slit along one side
- Four small plastic eggs or four eggs drawn on cardboard

Instructions
These puppets may be made with movable mouths or hands.

   Note: Bumble Bear needs a movable paw and should be made larger than the other puppets.

Puppets with movable mouths (See illustrations, p. 153.)

Supplies
Hooty Owl
- Dark, brown sock
- Cardboard for beak
- Yellow felt for beak
- Fringed felt or feathers for wings

Honey Bunny
- Light brown, grey, or white sock
- Cardboard for mouth
- Matching felt for ears (same as body)
- Pink felt for ears and nose
- Black felt or buttons for eyes
- Yarn for whiskers

Dog
- Brown, white, black, or grey sock
- Cardboard for mouth
- Matching felt for ear (same as body)
- Black felt or buttons for nose and eyes
- Red felt for tongue

Instructions
   1. Tuck the heel of the sock to make a straight tubular piece, fold down, and stitch.
   2. Cut the foot of the sock as shown by the dotted lines.

3. Turn the sock inside out and cut a piece of felt the shape of the mouth opening. Cut a matching mouth piece from cardboard. Sew the felt to the sock with an overhand stitch or use a sewing machine.

4. Turn sock right side out. Fold the cardboard piece in half and insert in the sock.

5. Add features such as eyes, nose, whiskers, ears. You may also add paws or wings by sewing them onto each side of the sock.

Puppets with movable arms (See illustrations, pp. 153-155.)
Supplies

Rocky Raccoon
- Two socks the same colour, grey or light brown
- Stuffing
- Yarn to tie around neck
- Marker for markings on face
- Black felt or buttons for nose, eyes, and ears

Bumble Bear
- Two extra-large socks the same colour, brown stuffing
- Yarn to tie around neck
- Brown felt for ears
- Black felt or buttons for nose and eyes

Instructions

1. Repeat step 1 of puppet with movable mouth. (See illustration.)

2. Insert stuffing up around the toe of the sock until head is plump and round, then tie yarn around the neck and stitch in place to keep it from slipping.

3. Cut toe from the second sock, turn inside out, and sew to a nose shape; stuff lightly, and stitch to the front of the head.

4. Make two small slits on either side of the body. Make two small paws from the second sock and sew over the slits at the sides of the puppet. Do not stuff because you will be using the paws with your fingers.

5. Add features such as eyes, ears, and nose.

Puppets with movable mouths

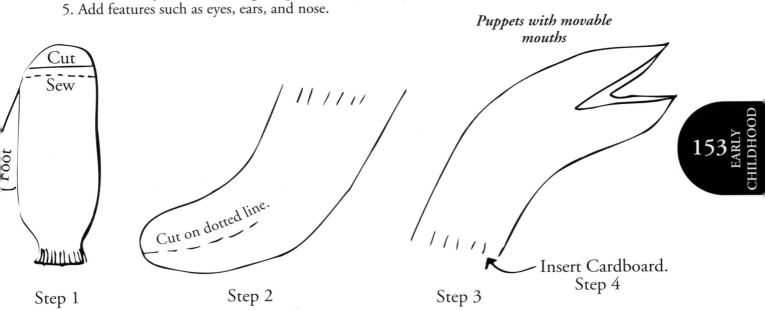

Cut

Sew

(foot)

Cut on dotted line.

Insert Cardboard.
Step 4

Step 1   Step 2   Step 3

Stuff head.

Step 2

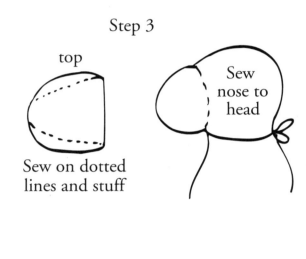

Step 3

top

Sew on dotted lines and stuff

Sew nose to head

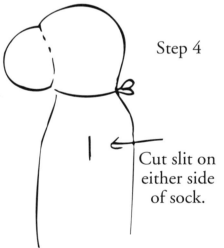

Step 4

Cut slit on either side of sock.

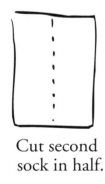

Cut second sock in half.

Roll lengthwise and sew sides together and bottom. Turn right side out and attach to sides of puppet.

Step 5

Add features.

Step 5

Add features.

Note: make bear larger than other puppets.

Songs

God's Family

Jesus and His Friends

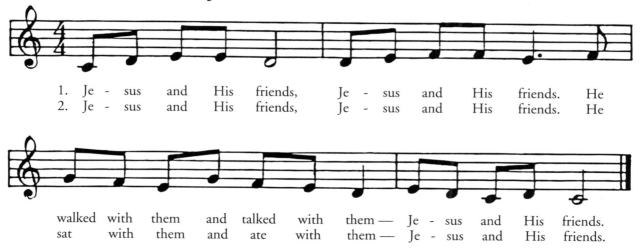

1. Je - sus and His friends, Je - sus and His friends. He
2. Je - sus and His friends, Je - sus and His friends. He

walked with them and talked with them — Je - sus and His friends.
sat with them and ate with them — Je - sus and His friends.

Words and music by Star Gipson

Jesus Listens When I Pray

Je - sus lis - tens when I pray, when I pray, when I pray.

Je - sus lis - tens when I pray, Ev - 'ry night, ev - 'ry day.

Words by Clara Ketelkut
Music by Arthur W. Gross, Arr. by J. C. Wohlfeil

Praise the Lord

1. Lit-tle chil-dren, praise the Lord, praise the Lord, praise the Lord.
2. Praise him for the Bi-ble true, Bi-ble true, Bi-ble true.

Lit-tle chil-dren, praise the Lord, praise — the Lord.
Praise him for the Bi-ble true, praise — the Lord.

The children may add other verses.

Charles Edward Polk, #156 *The Children's Hymnary*, © 1968 Faith & Life Press, Newton, KS 67114. Used by permission.

Together

Let's come to-geth - er now.____ Let's sing a song, our

heads we'll bow to talk to God, hear a sto - ry or two. There are

Repeat and fade away

lots of things to-geth - er we can do, to - geth - er,____ to -

geth - er,____ to - geth - er,____ to - geth - er,____

Words and music by Lois Redelfs Brokering

159 EARLY CHILDHOOD

Junior Youth

Junior Youth Introduction

These materials are for use with children in grades 6 through 8. The content complements the sections for kindergarten through grade 5. (See pages 31-112.)

Organization

1. The junior youth, ages eleven through thirteen (completed grades 6-8), will be part of the Worship that includes children in the kindergarten through grade 5. They should sit together as a separate group for the worship.

2. Junior youth may join the larger group for the Gather and Bless or may continue in their separate group.

3. The junior youth have their own 105-minute session. This time block includes Bible study and discussion, a break for snack and games, active responses, making a craft, and reflection.

Leadership

As a leader for this age, you should have a love for God and for adolescents who are beginning to search for an identity as young adults. Be an active listener, a discussion facilitator, an adult who is concerned for the natural and spiritual development of these youth. Model Christ-like living as you teach and interact with the youth. Be an advocate who helps them grow into a loving relationship with Jesus.

An invitation to faith is best offered as we adults "walk the talk," model a life of discipleship and joy, and talk about our relationship with Jesus Christ with sincerity and humility, remembering always that Jesus invites people in his own time and in his own way.

Study the Look it over (page 5) and Get it organized (page 11) sections. Check with the coordinator for general information about the curriculum.

Use the various resource sections listed in the Table of Contents to find the memory text, music, Bible story dramas, and games that are a part of each session plan.

Consider including the youth in the presentation of the Bible story dramas. The stories for Sessions 2 and 4 would be especially appropriate. Be a wind chorus for the Session 2 story. For Session 4, the group could play the part of the crowd. Check with the Worship coordinator to see how the junior youth might be involved.

Be aware of the needs and interests of your group. Change and adapt the material, keeping in mind the focus and theme for the week. Study the biblical background and text for each day. Reflect on your relationship with Jesus and what you can learn from Peter's story.

Characteristics of junior youth

Junior youth are moving into adolescence, a time of great change in their emotions and attitudes. A positive self-esteem is very important. Junior youth tend to worry about their looks, actions, feelings, acceptance by peers, parents, and other significant adults. Help them to feel accepted, comfortable, and positive about themselves. Provide an atmosphere of trust, mutual acceptance, and care.

Some junior youth are beginning to think about faith issues in a new way. As their skills in abstract thinking mature, they are able to question and reflect upon the Bible stories and God's activity in the world. They can begin to develop a more personal relationship with Jesus as a friend who will accept them and love them for who they are.

Junior youth are in that exciting stage of life between childhood and youth. As they mature toward adolescence and independence, they need adult models who can help them make the transition as smoothly as possible. Give them time and permission to explore faith-and-life issues at an age-appropriate level. Tell them that they are special and unique, and that you care about them.

Special items

Memory text

Distribute copies of the memory text to the junior youth to memorize. Use Gather and Greet or Gather and Bless for review. Encourage the youth to put the text to music or poetry to help them remember it. Spend time talking about the meaning of the text and how it illustrates transformed attitudes and behaviour.

Make a craft

Instructions for creating a mobile are suggested as an ongoing craft for the week. In the first session, youth will make a base for the mobile using wire and stone. Each day they are invited to design a symbol that represents the theme for that session. This symbol can be made during a regular craft time or during a personal reflection time at the end of the session. Have on hand a supply of art and craft materials as well as books with Christian symbols and banner ideas. This mobile is meant to be symbolic of the learning that has taken place. Encourage individuality and creativity in design, keeping in mind that God's invitation to discipleship happens in many different ways.

Additional activities

Have available several activities that youth can work on at their leisure.

1. Set up a sponge-painting area. Encourage youth to make pictures of the story that impressed them. Supply the area with paper, paints, brushes, and cleanup materials. The painting can be a mural for the week or a new picture for each day.

2. Set up a graffiti board for the youth to write slogans and phrases that have to do with following Jesus. This could be a chalkboard, bristol board,

wood, or newsprint. Consider letting the youth design a billboard with spray paint.

3. Set up a poetry or reading corner where youth can read about Bible times, read stories of people who followed Jesus, and write poems or songs. Check out your church library for books on Bible times and Bible lands. Set *Mirror of the Martyrs* (Good Books, 1990), a book about the early Anabaptists; books such as *Walking with Jesus*, Mary Clemens Myer (Herald Press, 1992); *Peace Be with You*, Cornelia Lehn (Faith and Life Press, 1980); and *I Heard Good News Today*, Cornelia Lehn (Faith and Life Press, 1983). Have paper and pencils available for writing.

Session plan

Use the times given as suggestions. Be flexible in the timing. Base your decisions on the maturity of the group, the size of the group, and the field trips or service projects you decide to do. Do not sacrifice the Bible study time. The Bible study sets the agenda for the response activity. The Bible study and response activity will have a long-lasting impact on the lives of the youth. Limit the group size to eight to ten youth to one teacher. Form additional groups as needed or team teach and share responsibilites for Bible study, discussion, and the various activities.

Gather and Greet (15 minutes)

Give the group a name that fits your group. Meet in a classroom or outside area.

Take attendance. Do group-building activities. Introduce the theme of the day and collect the offering.

Worship (30 minutes)

Attend Worship with the younger children or plan your own worship time. Sing songs that relate to the daily theme. Add favorites that the group knows. Listen to the Bible story drama presentation. Return to the Junior youth area for the following activities:

Study and Discuss (35 minutes)

Review the Bible story, interpret the story at a junior-youth level, and apply the truths learned to daily living. Provide Bibles for each youth so they can read the text each day. If possible, use a Bible translation that is easy to read, such as *The Good News Bible*.

Discuss Peter's characteristics as he grows in his relationship with his friend Jesus. Relate the biblical text to the experiences of youth through the exercises provided. Help the youth consider how Jesus can be a close friend to them. Pray that you and the Holy Spirit can guide these youth on an adventure with Jesus that will change their lives.

Take a Break (15 minutes)

Snack, relax, play some active games. Check the games in the Games and Snacks Resource, pages 81-96. These games correlate to the theme of each day.

Respond (40 minutes)

Junior youth have different learning preferences that need to be accommodated to hold their interest and attention. Some youth prefer to respond through hands-on activities such as crafts or games. Others learn best by thinking, writing, or drawing. Still others want to become involved in a project, such as helping at a nursing home, doing a service project, or touring a service agency.

Plan accordingly. Plan at least one field trip during the week. This will provide variety and help youth to put into practise Jesus' model of service to others. Consider the time factor and ask for written parental permission. Check insurance policies for transporting children, etc.

Reflect and Remember (15 minutes)

Invite the youth to think about the session's theme and how it applies to their own lives. Use this time for individual thinking, praying, writing, and/or creating the symbol for the mobile.

A letter from the Jesus response page is included for each session. This letter invites youth to think seriously about their relationship with Jesus as a friend. Space is provided on the letter for a personal response. Their response is to remain private. Encourage honesty and openness. This activity will appeal to youth who tend to be introspective and reflective.

If the group is not ready to spend this amount of time in silence, use the time for group reflection or for the creation of the symbol for the mobile. Suggest that each person sits in silence for a few minutes to think about the best symbol for them.

Gather and Bless (15 minutes)

You may choose to join the kindergarten through grade 5 group for singing and the closing blessing, or you may stay as a group for your own closure. Review the memory text, 2 Peter 1:3, 5-7. The Then and Now Resource, page 61, has creative ways to learn the memory text.

Session plans

Session 1

An Invitation to Follow: From Fisherman to Follower

Bible Text: Mark 1:16-20; Luke 5:1-11
Biblical Background: Mark 1:1-31
Story Focus: Peter was a fisherman who chose to give up his nets and his job to become a follower of Jesus. This was the beginning of a relationship with Jesus that would change his entire life.
Faith Focus: Jesus invites us to become his followers for life.

Gather and Greet

1. Choose a group name that fits the fishing/following theme for the week. Make name tags. As the youth arrive, let them use dark-coloured markers to print their names in the shape of a fish on a piece of bristol board (see logo, page 30). Cut out the shape; punch holes in the eye and the tail. Tie elastic thread to each hole to make an arm bracelet. Distribute name tags each day as the youth gather, and collect them at the end of each session.

2. Give each person a blank business-size envelope. Have them print their name on the front of the envelope. Use this envelope for the letters from Jesus that will be used during the reflection time each day. Set the signed envelopes aside. Sometime before Reflection time, insert the first letter into each envelope.

3. Do a group-building activity. As people complete their name tags, have them look up the meaning of their names in a book of names. Gather in a circle. Try these activities to learn each others' names:

   a. Give your complete name and preferred name. For example: "I am Susannah Deanne Hogan Smith. I'd like to be called Susie."

   b. Tell the group what your name means. If you do not know the meaning, tell the group what you think it could mean. Have the group tell what definitions come to mind with the sound of each name.

c. If the group is quite small, have each person give descriptions about themselves along with their names. Use alliterative adjectives to provide the descriptions. First use one adjective (energetic Eleanor). Continue around the circle, adding silly and serious descriptions all beginning with the first sound of the first letter of the name.

4. Pray together before you go to Worship. Invite God to be present with each one as they learn about following Jesus. Go with the junior youth to the worship area. Stay with the group and model active participation.

Worship

See page 34.

Study and Discuss

1. Begin with a focusing activity that will help the youth connect with Peter as a person who had real decisions to make about his life and his relationship with Jesus. They will learn that following Jesus means a change in attitude, behaviour, and character, and involves risk and uncertainties.

Play *The Choice is Yours!* Have everyone stand in the centre of the room. If you are outside, set up rope markers 15 feet, 5 meters, apart. Ask group members to move to one side or the other in response to each question. There are no right or wrong answers. Each person will make a decision based on her/his feelings and preferences. However, no one is allowed to remain in the centre (neutral)–all must make a choice. Here are some questions to ask them:

- Would you choose pizza or hamburgers for lunch?
- Would you choose to play baseball or watch others play baseball?
- Would you choose to own purple or black gym shoes?
- Would you choose to watch television or read a book?
- Would you choose to have a high-paying job or help others for free?
- Would you choose to go to camp by yourself or with friends?
- Would you choose to travel to a familiar place or go some place new?
- Would you choose to have one best friend or several good friends?
- Would you choose to be a leader or a follower?
- Would you choose to have an adult friend or a youth friend act as your guide on a trip to another part of the world?

2. Discuss. Gather in the centre to talk about the choices that were made. Which choices were easy to make? Why? Which decisions were more difficult to make? Why? How did you feel about the choices you had to make? Did the choices others made influence your decision? What did you learn about yourself through this exercise? What did you learn about others?

Tie the discussion into Peter's choices.

- What choices did Peter have to make?
- How do you think he arrived at his decision to leave his fishing nets and follow Jesus?

3. Study the Bible. Distribute chart paper, markers, and Bibles. Divide into groups of about four persons. Half of the groups will read Mark 1:16-20 and the other half will read Luke 5:1-11.

Have the following assignment written on large index cards:

a. Read the story from the Bible.

b. What questions do you think Peter had about following Jesus?

c. Make a list of possible reasons Peter might give to follow Jesus.

d. Make another list of reasons he might use to remain a fisherman.

e. Why do you think he immediately followed Jesus?

f. What did you learn about Peter from this story?

g. What did you learn about Jesus from this story?

Ask each group to report briefly to the rest of the group. Make a collective list of the reasons for following or not following Jesus that Peter might have used. (See illustration.) Begin to develop a character sketch of Peter and Jesus. Have a piece of chart paper entitled "Peter is . . ." and one with "Jesus is . . ." Each day add words that describe Peter and Jesus based on the Bible stories.

4. Bring closure to the discussion. Ask the youth to think quietly about the reasons they have for choosing to follow Jesus. Encourage them to think about the choices they will make about many things in life.

Explain that this week will be a time to explore together what it means to have a growing relationship with Jesus. Tell them you will listen to any questions they have about God and Jesus and will share your own experiences and thoughts about following Jesus.

5. Close with prayer, inviting Jesus to be the group's guide and friend during your week together.

Take a Break

1. Have a simple snack.

2. Play *Crazy Relay*. See page 85, Games and Snacks Resource.

3. Instead of the game, set up an obstacle course that requires partner assistance. Use this exercise to illustrate that Jesus wants to help us on our journey through life.

Respond

1. Make a base for the mobile. If you choose to do the ongoing craft, have the youth prepare the bases as well as design the first symbols. (See page 169.)

Supplies

- One stone per person, the size of a closed fist
- Acrylic paints, paintbrushes or permanent markers
- Sturdy wire and wire cutters (may use wire clothes hangers)
- Small pieces of felt
- Glue
- Heavy cardboard, bristol board, or wood for a sturdy base (optional)

Instructions

a. Choose a stone.

b. Cut a piece of wire long enough to fit around the stone and form the shape of an upright cross. Either wrap the wire around the stone or make a horizontal circle in which the stone will nestle. Form the rest of the wire into a cross shape.

c. Glue a piece of felt to the bottom of the stone to prevent scratching on other surfaces. As an option, glue the felt to the underside of the cardboard or all around it to add colour to the base.

    d. Print your name onto the front of the stone in clear, large letters using markers or paints. Set aside to dry.

2. Make a mobile symbol. Invite youth to make a small symbol to remind them of the theme each session. Encourage creativity and individuality. Today's theme, "An Invitation to Follow," can be illustrated by using a variety of symbols.

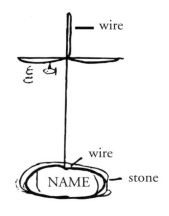

    a. *Footprints:* Make a set of sandals or shoes as a symbol of our willingness to walk with Jesus. Use construction paper, pieces of leather, etc., to form the footwear. Join pieces together with a piece of thin shoelace and hang over the bar on the cross.

    b. *Fish Symbol:* The fish shape was used extensively by early Christians as a secret symbol of following Jesus. People would mark the symbol in the dirt with a sandal or stick so that others would know that it was safe to talk about Jesus. The Greek word for "fish," *ichthus,* contains the initial letters of the words that described Jesus: "Jesus, Christ, God's, Son, Saviour."

As a fisherman, Peter made the decision to give up his nets in favour of catching "people." Make a small fish symbol using one of these ideas or your own: origami paper folding, or write a poem in the shape of a fish and cut around it. See *Becoming God's Peacemakers,* Living Stones Collection, page 75 (Faith & Life Press: Newton, Kans., 1992), for directions to make an origami fish.

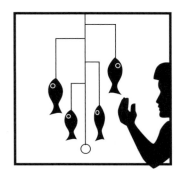

Attach the fish symbol to the cross with thread or fishing line.

3. Make a fish mobile. Attach fish of various shapes and sizes to a mobile frame. Hang from the ceiling. See illustration.

Reflect and Remember

1. Provide a quiet, reflective atmosphere. Encourage each youth to find a quiet spot and to think about the session's theme and what it means. Hand out the envelopes with the letter from Jesus. Suggest that they think about the words in a personal way and respond by talking to Jesus as a friend or by writing a letter to him on the other side of the page. Remind the group that this is "alone with Jesus" time and no one will see what is written unless they choose to share it.

2. Gather together for a closing prayer.

Gather and Bless

1. Begin to learn the Bible memory passage, 2 Peter 1:3, 5-7. See pages 62-68.

2. Explain to the group what your closing ritual will be. Choose a group theme song, Scripture text, sentence prayer, or some other meaningful way to end your time together every day. Encourage group members to invite others to join the adventure with Peter and Jesus this week.

3. Give any necessary instructions before you dismiss the group.

Peter's Choices to Follow Jesus

Yes	No
☑ _____	☒ _____
_____	_____
_____	_____
_____	_____
☑ _____	☒ _____
_____	_____
_____	_____
_____	_____
☑ _____	☒ _____
_____	_____
_____	_____
_____	_____
☑ _____	☒ _____
_____	_____
_____	_____
_____	_____
☑ _____	☒ _____
_____	_____
_____	_____
_____	_____

Dear Friend,

How are you? I am sending you this letter to tell you how much I love you and care for you. I want to be your best friend, just like I was Simon Peter's best friend. I have known you since you were a tiny baby and have watched you grow into a fine young person. I have been happy for you when you have fun with your friends and family. I have been sad for you when things did not go as you planned.

I want you to join me on an adventure of life. I will be your guide. I will show you the way. I will be with you to laugh with you, to cry with you, to grow with you. Come with me and be my friend. This is the same invitation I gave to Peter: "Follow me."

Think about it before you decide. Talk to me about it. Ask me questions. It's your decision. Remember, no matter what you decide, I love you. I have chosen you, and because of this I will wait for you. I want you to be my friend.

Your friend, Jesus

Dear Jesus,,

Session 2

An Invitation to Faith: From Faith to Failure to Faith

> **Bible Text:** Matthew 14:22-33
> **Story Focus:** Peter's initial faith in Jesus faltered when he attempted to walk on the water to meet Jesus. After Jesus rescued him, Peter and the disciples believed that Jesus was God's special son.
> **Faith Focus:** When we focus on Jesus, we can do more than we think we can.

Gather and Greet

1. Distribute name tags. Welcome newcomers to class with a personal greeting and introductions to the group. Be sure to give each newcomer a name tag and an envelope to sign.

2. Talk about trust. What does it mean? Whom do you trust the most? Why do you trust some people and not others? How have you experienced trust? Invite them to look for ways the characters show trust in the Bible story.

3. Go with the group to Worship. Encourage full participation of all junior youth in the worship time.

Worship

See page 37.

Study and Discuss

1. Review the Bible story through creative drama and experiencing a "trust walk." Help youth begin to understand what it means to have faith in Jesus

through the ordinary and the difficult situations in life.

Do the Bible story drama "Peter on the Sea." Retell the story using the "tableau" format. Youth demonstrate their feelings with posture and facial expression. This activity requires imagination and expression of feelings.

a. Ask each youth to find a spot apart from others.

b. Distribute Bibles and have each youth read Matthew 14:22-33 silently.

c. Ask them to try to imagine the feelings and thoughts they might have had as a disciple of Jesus.

d. Set the Bibles aside.

For each scene that follows, give instructions and invite individual responses through pantomime.

a. While the scene is being read, have the youth form their responses.

b. Then call "Freeze!" and everyone stops all movement.

c. After a few seconds, tell the group to relax the pose but to stay in character.

d. Move on to the next scene.

Note: If you have a camcorder, you can videotape the "frozen" pictures for all to look at later.

Peter on the Sea

Scene One

Settle in your boat for the trip across the lake. It has been a long exhausting day. You are tired and anxious to get home. You are sad because Jesus did not come with you. As you row, you begin to notice that the wind has picked up and you are being pushed out to sea. How do you react to this? Show with your body and your face. [*Pause*] Freeze! [*Pause*] Relax.

Scene Two

The storm starts to get worse. [*Pause as youth get "into the story" again.*] Look over there! There is someone or something out there! It looks as if someone is walking toward you. What do you do? Show with your face and your body. [*Pause*] Freeze! [*Pause*] Relax.

Scene Three

You realize that it might be Jesus coming toward you. You call to him. Yes, it is Jesus. He tells you to not be afraid. You calm down. Then you get an idea. If Jesus can walk on the water, maybe you can too. Take the risk. Step out of the boat and begin to walk toward Jesus. How does it feel to be walking on the water? How do you express your feelings? [*Pause*] Freeze! [*Pause*] Relax.

Scene Four

You continue walking toward Jesus. Suddenly you realize what is happening and you begin to sink in the water. In desperation you call to Jesus to save you from drowning. Jesus comes toward you, reaching out his hands to grab you. Capture the expression of being rescued by Jesus. [*Pause*] Freeze! [*Pause*] Relax.

Scene Five

Walk with Jesus back to your boat. Climb into the boat. How do you show your relief that you are safe? How do you worship Jesus as the Son of God? [*Pause*] Freeze! [*Pause*] Relax.

Debrief. Have the group tell about their thoughts and feelings. Ask questions like: Was it easy or difficult to think and feel as Peter did? Why? How would you describe the different feelings you had? What did you learn about Peter? What did you learn about trust or faith in Jesus?

Add the character traits that the group discovered about Peter and Jesus to the charts begun in Session 1.

2. Do a trust walk activity called *Lighthouse* to help youth experience trust. Each person will need a partner. The setting for this activity requires ample space for walking and a few obstacles. If you are indoors, you will walk from one wall to another. If outdoors, set up two ropes about 30 feet, 10 meters, apart for end zones.

    a. Partners line up along one wall.

    b. For the first walk, Partner A of each team will guide partner B across the room *without talking*. Hands can be used. It is up to Partner A to guide partner B safely across to the other side, avoiding other pairs and the obstacles.

    c. For the return walk, Partner A will guide Partner B back to the starting point with voice only and *without touching*.

    d. Exchange roles and repeat this activity with the same partners.

When you are finished with the trust walks, gather together for a brief discussion about this experience. If the group is large, divide into groups of five or six, each with an adult to guide the discussion. Ask questions such as these:

- What happened?
- What feelings did you have?
- Did you prefer being the guide (partner A) or the guided (partner B)? Why?
- What did you learn about yourself?
- What did you learn about others?
- How was this activity like Peter's experience on the water?
- What did this activity tell you about God and faith/trust?
- How would you define faith in God in your own words?
- When do you need to have faith in Jesus?
- How can Jesus help you face the scary times in your life? How can Jesus help you face your fears?

3. Close in prayer, thanking God for being our guide when we do not always know where we are going.

Take a Break

1. Have a simple snack.
2. Play one of the games found in the Games and Snacks Resource, page 87-88.

Respond

Choose from the following activities that are appropriate for the interests of your group and possible in your setting:

1. Conduct faith interviews. Arrange to visit individuals in your community who have a faith story to share with junior youth. Choose people who have experienced many difficulties in their lives and have maintained a strong faith in God. Visit one or two people. Have the youth prepare and ask them questions about how God helped them in their difficult times.

Note:
- Take your snack to share with the people being interviewed.
- If your group is large and you have several vehicles, interview different

individuals. When you return, share your experiences with each other.

• Rather than travel for these interviews, invite persons to come to you.

2. Plan a service project or tour of a place in your community where people are serving. Visit a local church-sponsored service agency (SELFHELP or SERRV Crafts, soup kitchen, Mennonite Central Committee, or your mission office, thrift shop, counseling centre, etc.) Invite people at these agencies to tell how their faith in God prompted them to serve the community. Tour the facilities to learn how they operate.

Offer to give volunteer assistance if possible. Arrange ahead of time for hands-on projects that the youth can do during their visit.

3. Make a craft. See Make and Take Resource, pages 106-107. Or choose a craft that will illustrate the concept of faith. Spend time talking about possible symbols for the mobile began in Session 1. Use this time rather than the personal reflection time to design the mobile symbol.

Reflect and Remember

1. Encourage each youth to think about the theme, "From Faith to Failure to Faith." Have a variety of materials on hand for the mobile symbol (paper, plastic, Styrofoam meat trays, scissors, glue, sequins, pipe cleaners). Make a symbol to add to the mobile begun in Session 1.

2. Distribute the letter from Jesus, page 176. Invite youth to think about the message and write a responding letter to Jesus.

3. Gather together for a closing prayer.

Gather and Bless

1. Conduct your closing rituals. The chorus of the song "Put Your Hand in the Hand of the Man" (Gene MacLellan) well reflects the theme of the day. Sing it or another appropriate song together.

2. Continue Bible memory. (See pages 62-68.)

3. Give each youth a word of encouragement as they leave.

Dear Jesus,,

Dear Friend,

How are you today? How does it feel to know that you are loved by me? Do you ever find yourself in a situation like Peter found himself? Do you sometimes get scared about what is happening around you? Peter took a risk and became very frightened. But I was there to grab hold of his hand and lead him to safety. He trusted me and all was well.

Will you trust me to help you in times of trouble? What are your fears? Tell me about your problems. I am ready to listen to you, to give you my undivided attention, because I love you and I care very much for you.

When things are not going well for you, reach out to me. I will be there for you in the scary times. Trust me. You can count on me. I will help you face your fears.

I love you. I want you to trust me as your very best friend.

Your friend, Jesus

Session 3

An Invitation to Loyalty: From Loyalty to Betrayal

Bible Texts: John 13:34-38; Mark 14:66-72
Biblical Background: John 13:1-38; John 18:1-11; Luke 22:51; John 19:1—20:1-23.
Story Focus: Peter wanted to be a loyal friend to Jesus, but when frightening things that he did not understand began to happen, he denied the friendship. Even though Peter did not pass the loyalty test, Jesus continued to love him.
Faith Focus: It is easy to slip back into old patterns of behaviour when we are faced with new and frightening situations. Jesus continues to love and forgive us even when we do not act like his friend.

Gather and Greet

1. Greet each person individually. Welcome any newcomers.
2. Distribute name tags.
3. Ask the youth to name the most important quality of a friend. Have them look for qualities of friendship during Worship.
4. Go to Worship as a group.

Worship

See page 40.

Study and Discuss

1. Help the youth consider the qualities of a good friendship and what it means for them to build a friendship with Jesus.
2. Make a Friendship Report Card for Peter. Distribute a Bible, a pencil, and a copy of Peter's report card (page 185) to each person.

a. Have youth read the texts listed in the Biblical Background, page 177. You may wish to divide the text into smaller sections and have individuals read silently and summarize orally for the group before they complete the report cards.

b. Have the youth individually circle the grades they would give Peter. How would they grade him overall as a friend?

c. Discuss responses using these questions as starters:
- In which areas did Peter fail miserably?
- Which do you think was his "worst" failure as a friend?
- Would you accept Peter as your friend? Why or why not?
- What rating would Peter have to have in order to remain your friend?
- What rating would Peter have to have in order to still be a friend to Jesus?
- How would you rate Jesus as a friend to Peter?

d. Ask the group members to complete the report card for themselves. What kind of a friend are they? How do they rate their friendship with Jesus?

3. Do role-plays. See Friendship Dilemmas (page 180). Distribute one dilemma to each pair. Make several copies of the dilemmas so there are enough for each pair.

a. Work with a partner to discuss and resolve each dilemma.

b. Decide on the issue of friendship that is being addressed.

c. Consider the choices that could be made.

d. Prepare and conduct a conversation that would show how the two people can become friends again.

After the dilemmas have all been presented, talk about the meaning of friendship for the youth. Encourage them to tell about times when they were disappointed in a friend or when they may have disappointed a friend because of something they did or said.

Remind the youth that Jesus is a friend who is always with us, who understands our thoughts and feelings, and who will always be there for us.

4. Close with a time of guided silent prayer. Invite youth to think about a time that they hurt a friend. Ask God to forgive them. Think of a time they have been hurt by a friend. Ask God to forgive them. Talk to Jesus about your friendship. Close with a prayer of thanks to God for listening to our prayers and for being a good friend.

Take a Break

1. Have a simple snack.

2. Play *Blanket Ball Toss,* a cooperative game. See Games and Snacks Resource, page 90.

Respond

Choose one of the following activities:

1. Make friendship bracelets to symbolize loyalty between two people. Use the directions on page 182. Let these bracelets be symbols of each person's desire to be friends with Jesus. The fish design in the bracelet can remind youth of the special relationship they have with Jesus when they become his loyal followers.

Supplies

- Directions (page 182)
- Embroidery floss, at least two contrasting colours per person
- Safety pins

Instructions

a. Cut the floss in 48 inches, 120 centimeters, lengths. Each person will need six lengths of the dominant colour and two lengths of the contrasting colour.

b. Follow instructions on the pattern.

Note: You will not be able to complete this project in one day. Decide beforehand if you wish to continue this craft in Session 4 or send it home for completion.

Option: Make a mini-bracelet for the mobile. Follow Steps 1 through 3 and only complete one fish in the design.

2. Make wall plaques. Use the design (page 184).

a. Trace the design onto heavy poster board or other material.

b. Use Exacto knives to cut out the shape.

Note: If you choose to use wood for the plaque, be very careful with the cutting tools. Find an expert woodworker to lead this craft.

Reflection and Remember

1. Reflect on the session's theme of loyalty and friendship.

2. Make mobile symbols to reflect the theme. Consider a simple braided piece of the embroidery floss used for the friendship bracelets.

3. Distribute the letter from Jesus and encourage a written response.

4. Gather together for a closing prayer.

Gather and Bless

Close with your usual rituals, Bible memory review, and blessing.

Friendship Dilemmas

Photocopy these dilemmas. Cut the strips apart. Have enough copies of each dilemma so that the youth can work in pairs.

- Monique and Erika have been best friends for several years. A cute guy named Ben has moved into the neighbourhood and is in their class in school. Both girls like Ben very much. Ben begins to show a special interest in Erika. What is the friendship issue here? How can the girls remain close friends?

- Brad and Jeff are best friends. Brad confided to Jeff that he sometimes cries when he watches a sad TV show. One day, after an argument with Brad, Jeff told another friend that Brad is a crybaby. Brad found this out. What is the friendship issue here? How can Brad and Jeff continue to be friends?

- Kimberly and Stacy have become good friends at school. Stacy likes to spend time at Kim's house, but Stacy never invites her to her home. When Kimberly begs to see her friend's home, Stacy tells her that her mother is an alcoholic and yells at her. She is too embarrassed to invite Kim in. What is the friendship issue here? How will Kimberly react to her friend's home situation?

- Raphael and Rene have been friends for a long time. Raphael really enjoys sports, while Rene prefers to play computer games. One will participate with the other because they enjoy being together. Shil, a new boy in town, has joined the soccer team and become friends with Raphael. Rene is afraid that Raphael would rather be with Shil than with him. What is the friendship issue here? How can this dilemma be resolved?

- Chris and Terry are good friends and classmates. Chris failed the last math test. Terry overhears some other friends talking about how stupid Chris is. What is the friendship issue here? How can Terry be a good friend?

- Dave and Luke are best friends. Both are active and like to plan things to go their way. One day they get into an argument about whether to go swimming or bowling. This argument ends in a physical fight and both stomp home feeling sorry for themselves. What is the friendship issue here? How can they become friends again?

- Dale and Ashley are good friends. They are often at each other's homes and enjoy each other's families. Ashley's father has AIDS and is slowly dying. What is the friendship issue here? How can Dale be a good friend to Ashley?

- Rick and Ron have just become friends. Ron has not had too many friends and is very happy that Rick, who is new in town, wants to be his friend. While at the corner store, Ron sees Rick slip a few chocolate bars into his jacket pocket. Both Ron and Rick buy ice cream cones, but Rick leaves the store without paying for the chocolate bars. What is the friendship issue here? What does Ron say to Rick?

Permission is granted to photocopy this page.

Dear Jesus,,

Dear Friend,

How are you today? Did you like Peter's story? You know, Peter made me very sad that day. I thought he would be a loyal friend. I knew that he was short-tempered and impatient sometimes. But even though I was disappointed in Peter's actions, I still loved him very much. I was disappointed, but that did not stop me from caring for him.

Sometimes your actions and attitudes disappoint me, too. I know it is hard for you to do the right thing all the time. It makes me sad to be let down, but I understand. I will not hold it against you. I will forgive you when you ask, just as I forgave Peter.

Just remember, I will always love you and forgive you, because I am your friend. I am here to listen to you and to talk to you about our friendship. Just call on me and I will answer.

Your friend, Jesus

181

Friendship Bracelet

Use the embroidery floss.

Tie the strands together leaving a 2 to 2 1/2-inch, 5 to 6.25-centimeter, tail. Put a safety pin through the knot and secure to a stable surface (a small pillow works well). A clipboard may also be used. Smooth out the strands so the two contrasting color strands are on the outside. (See Diagram A.)

Note: Before you begin, study Diagrams B and C. These are the stitches that are used to make the bracelet. Each "stitch" is actually two knots. Always make two knots in succession. Also be careful not to pull the embroidery floss too hard. The bracelet may flip over and the wrong color will be exposed.

Step 1: Knotted Loop (for tying bracelet)

1. Take String A and stitch onto strings A1, A2, then A3. Now A1 should be on the outside.

2. Stitch A1, A2, A3, then A. A2 should be on the outside.

3. Stitch A2 on A3, A, then A. A3 should be on the outside.

4. Stitch A3 on A, A1, then A2. Now A should be on the outside once again.

5. The same is done with Side B. Stitch B onto B1, B2, then B3. Follow the instructions for Side A (1-4), but remember to use the backwards L-shape stitch (see Diagram C).

6. Your bracelet should now look like Diagram D.

Step 2: Fish Design–Tail

1. Stitch String A on A1, A2, then A3. String A should be in the middle.

2. Stitch String B on B1, B2, then B3. String B should be in the middle.

3. Connect A and B using the L-shape stitch (see Diagram B). This knot will close the loop that was made.

4. The bracelet should now look like Diagram E.

Step 3: Fish Design–Body

1. Stitch A1 on A2, then A3. Stitch B1 on B2, then B3.

2. Stitch A2 on A3. Stitch B2 on B3.

3. The bracelet should now look like Diagram F.

4. Stitch String B over to the left using the backwards L-shape stitch so it is on the outside (on A1, A2, then A3).

5. Stitch String A over to the right using the L-shape stitch so it is on the outside (on B1, B2, then B3).

6. Stitch the two center strings (A1 and B1) together using the L-shape stitch (see Diagram B).

7. Stitch B1 on A2, then A3. Stitch A1 on B2, then B3.

8. Stitch two center strands (A2 and B2).

9. Stitch A3 on B2. Stitch B3 on A2.

10. Stitch two center strands (A3 and B3).

11. Stitch B over to the right (on B1, B2, then B3) and A over to the left (on A1, A2, then A3) so A and B are in the middle. Stitch A and B together.

12. Check the design. The first fish should now be complete (see Diagram G).

Step 4: Dividing the Fish Designs

1. Stitch A1 on A2, A3, then A.

2. Stitch B1 on B2, B3, then B.

3. Tie center strands.

4. Continue stitching outside strands to the center until String A and String B are on the outside. Always remember to stitch center strands or bracelet will separate (see Diagram H).

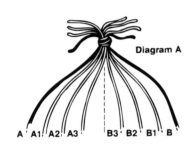

Diagram A

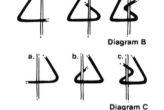

Diagram B

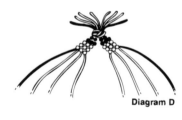

Diagram C

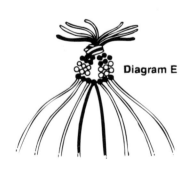

Diagram D

Diagram E

5. Go back to **Step 2: Fish Design–Tail**. Repeat Steps 2-4 until bracelet fits comfortably around wrist.

Step 5: Finishing

1. To finish the bracelet, take the outside strand from Side A and stitch until the center strand is reached. Now use the same strand and stitch it towards the outside once again. Continue this back and forth pattern several times (the bracelet should be separating like it did in the beginning section). Then repeat the pattern with Side B.

2. Braid the remaining threads from Side A and tie together, then braid Side B and tie together.

3. Cut off remaining loose threads.

4. The bracelet is now complete (see Diagram I).

Important

1. Attach a label to the end of each strand to identify as shown in Diagram A.

2. After stitching on a strand, immediately move it out of the way so it does not interfere with the other strands.

3. When moving to the left, always use the backwards L-shape stitch. When moving to the right, always use the L-shape stitch. When joining center strands together, always use the L-shape stitch.

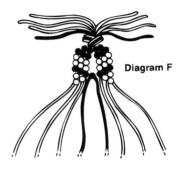

Diagram F

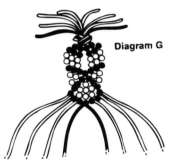

Diagram G

Diagram H

Diagram I

Permission is granted to photocopy this page.

Name_____

Marked by _____

FRIENDSHIP REPORT CARD

Can be trusted	A	B	C	D	E
Is loyal	A	B	C	D	E
Is a good listener	A	B	C	D	E
Can be counted on	A	B	C	D	E
Follows Jesus' way of peace and nonviolence	A	B	C	D	E
Present in times of trouble	A	B	C	D	E
Does what a friend requests	A	B	C	D	E
Stands up for a friend	A	B	C	D	E
Is truthful	A	B	C	D	E
Takes risks for a friend	A	B	C	D	E

Rating

A - the best friend one could ever have

B - a good friend

C - an "OK" friend who might disappoint you

D - undependable, not really a friend

E - a real loser

What grade do you give Peter as a friend to Jesus?

What grade would you give yourself?

Session 4

An Invitation to Courage: From Fear to Courage

Bible Text: Acts 2:1-42
Story Focus: At Pentecost, God's Spirit changed Peter from a fearful follower to a courageous leader. Peter was no longer afraid to tell others about Jesus when he realized that the Holy Spirit was helping him.
Faith Focus: When we let God's Holy Spirit live in us, we are given courage to act boldly for Jesus.

Gather and Greet

1. Greet each person. Distribute name tags.

2. To prepare for the theme of the day, ask each person to think about and complete this sentence: "It would take a whole lot of courage for me to...." Do not discuss or question their responses. Encourage each person to be honest and sensitive about each other's fears. Ask the group to look for Peter's solution to facing fears in the Bible story.

3. Go together to Worship.

Worship

See page 43.

Study and Discuss

Help the youth learn about the third person of the Trinity, God's Holy Spirit. Use the Scripture study and discussion to help them discover how the Holy Spirit changed Peter's life and how the Holy Spirit can be a transforming presence in their lives.

1. Begin with a focusing activity, "Who is this Holy Spirit?" Distribute

balloons of all shapes and sizes. Have the youth feel the balloons, stretch them, and make comments about their usefulness in their flat, airless form. Then have them blow up their balloons and knot them. Talk about the changes in the balloons when filled with air. How does this balloon exercise remind us of the story of Pentecost? Set the balloons aside.

Based on the Bible story presentation of the Pentecost experience, lead a discussion. Encourage and value their serious comments and thoughts.
- How would youth describe the Holy Spirit?
- How does the Holy Spirit look, act, and influence people?

2. Distribute Bibles and read the biblical account of Pentecost and its effect on Peter (Acts 2:1-24, 32-33, 36-42). Consider these questions:
- How was Peter changed by the Holy Spirit?
- How were other people changed by the Holy Spirit?
- What did you learn about Peter?

Add the characteristics that describe Peter to the Peter's Choices chart (see page 170).

3. Discover what the Holy Spirit does. The Holy Spirit was promised to the people long before Pentecost. The prophet Joel promised the gift of the Spirit to all people. Jesus promised to send one who would act on his behalf when he no longer lived on the earth.

Write the following texts on slips of paper and have the youth read the Scriptures to discover what the Holy Spirit can do for believers. Make a list together.
- John 14:16, 17 (advocate or comforter)
- John 16:13-15 (teacher and guide)
- John 16:8-11 (convicts of wrongdoing)
- 1 Corinthians 12:4-7 (gives gifts for the common good)
- Galatians 5:18 (leads)
- Galatians 5:22-26 (produces results)

Place this list of what the Spirit does beside the chart of Jesus' characteristics. See Session 1 Study and Discuss #3, page 167.

Discuss how Jesus and the Holy Spirit are alike–how are they different. Remind the youth that the Holy Spirit continues to do these things today. We can rely on the Spirit to comfort, teach, guide, convict, give spiritual gifts, and empower us. The Spirit is a gift from God to help us follow Jesus.

4. Sing songs about the Holy Spirit. Check your hymnal or ask your youth choir director for suggestions. Include favourites the group knows.

5. Pray together, inviting the Holy Spirit to give courage to the youth to speak and act boldly for Jesus.

Take a Break

1. Have a simple snack.
2. Play the game *Bubble Over*. See Games and Snacks Resource, page 89. After the game, ask these questions:
- What happened with your bubbles?
- Was it easy or hard getting the bubble to blow?
- How did you feel about having to start over?
- A symbol for the Holy Spirit is the wind. What did this game teach you about the Holy Spirit?
- What did you learn about yourself and your relationship with the Holy Spirit?

Respond

Choose from the following options. Make your decision based on the skills and interests of your group and the proximity of places to visit.

1. Complete the friendship bracelet from Session 3 or do another related craft. See the Make and Take Resource, pages 108-109. Or use this time to make the symbol for the mobile (see Reflect and Remember, page 189).

2. Participate in a service project. Peter was a changed person after the Holy Spirit became part of his life. He no longer was afraid to tell others about Jesus and his friendship with him. He wanted everyone to know that he was a follower. What can your group do that can be a witness to God's love and power? What are the needs in your own neighbourhood?

- Sing Christian songs and/or read favourite Scripture texts to older people in a nursing home or seniors' residence.
- Visit the home of an elderly or disabled person to clean windows or rake the lawn. Be sure to explain why you are helping out.
- Make cards that express Jesus' love for others and hand deliver them with hugs to someone in the community that might benefit from such attention.
- Deliver church brochures to homes around your church and personally invite families to worship at your church.
- Collect canned goods or used toys from people in your neighbourhood and deliver these items to a service agency. (If you do this, alert the neighbourhood beforehand so that they are expecting the youth.)

After the service project, talk about how the youth felt when they could share the good news about Jesus. Encourage them to tell others about their friendship with Jesus. Remind them that God has promised that the Holy Spirit will help them have the courage to speak.

3. Play games that illustrate transformed living. After each game is played, talk about how it fits with the day's theme. If you choose this option, shorten the **Take a Break** for snack only and use the game *Bubble Over* here.

Game 1: *Bubble Over.* (See page 89.)

Game 2: *Caterpillar\Butterfly.* Set up an obstacle course outside using cars, trees, tires, chairs, etc. Each person will complete the course two times. First, they must travel over the course by crawling on hands and knees (caterpillar). If the course is not suitable for crawling, have them squat down with their hands around their ankles. On the second round, have them complete the course in the upright position (butterfly).

After everyone has completed the course, sit in a circle and discuss these questions:

- Was it easier to move as a caterpillar or as a butterfly?
- How did you feel as a caterpillar? as a butterfly?
- How did the Holy Spirit change Peter from a caterpillar to a butterfly?
- What can this game tell us about our lives and the Holy Spirit?
- What are "caterpillar" activities for junior youth?
- What are "butterfly" activities for youth?

4. Read a book about transforming lifestyles such as *Hope for the Flowers*, Trina Paulus (Paulist Press, 1972). *Hope for the Flowers* is a story about two caterpillars whose hope for a better life transformed them completely. Talk about the transformations that happen in attitudes, looks, and actions. Check your church or local library for a copy of this book.

Reflect and Remember

1. Think quietly about today's theme of empowerment by the Holy Spirit.

2. Distribute the personal letter from Jesus and invite a written response.

3. Design a symbol of the Spirit for the mobile using symbols that are used to describe the Holy Spirit (such as a dove, fire, wind) and coloured streamers. Again have a supply of materials on hand for the mobile symbol. Some suggestions are: tongues of fire from coloured construction paper, mini-streamers out of tissue paper, a wind symbol such as a pinwheel or a spiral, a white descending dove. Check the church library for pattern books with Christian symbols.

Gather and Bless

Close with your usual ritual, Bible memory, and the blessing.

Dear Jesus,,

Dear Friend,

How are you today? Did you like the "new" Peter in today's story? He certainly became a changed person when he met the Holy Spirit, didn't he? He became the leader I hoped he would. You know, I sent the Holy Spirit to Peter and the other followers because I loved them and could not be with them in person. We work together to encourage people to be brave and strong.

We can help you, too. When you are unsure of what to say or do, call on me. Tell me all about it. I can give you courage to tell others about me. That's what friends are for, to encourage each other. Let my Spirit live in you and fill you with God's love. Let my Spirit transform you.

I love you, my friend.

Your friend, Jesus

Permission is granted to photocopy this page.

Session 5

An Invitation to Acceptance: From Rejection to Acceptance

Bible Text: Acts 10:1-48
Story Focus: After a vision from God, Peter believed that it was not right for him to be prejudiced against people who were not Jews. All people are accepted equally by God.
Faith Focus: When we think like God, we value all people as God does.

Gather and Greet

1. Distribute name tags if they are still needed.

2. As preparation for the Bible story and theme, review the stories about Peter. Read the titles of each session's theme, noting the changes in Peter's character each day. Tell the group that there is one more change that needs to happen in Peter's character. Invite the group to guess what that change might be.

Worship

See page 47.

Study and Discuss

Encourage youth to examine their own attitudes toward others who are different from themselves. They will realize that following Jesus is an ongoing process—we are continually being transformed or changed into Christlikeness.

1. Do a friendship checklist. Distribute the Friendship Checklist (page 195), pencils, and Bibles. Allow time for the youth to think about their

friends and to complete the checklist. After the checklists are completed, ask the group to think about their choice of friends. Discuss the following:
- Do your friends have a similar family background as you do?
- Do your friends have the same religious beliefs and values?
- Do your friends have the same abilities as you do?
- What personal rules do you have for making a new friend?
- What kind of person would you prefer *not* to have for a friend?
- What did you learn about yourself in this exercise?

2. Study the Bible to find out what Peter learned about accepting and rejecting people who were different from him. Review the Bible story of Peter's acceptance of Cornelius as a believer. Talk about the attitudes Peter had about associating with a person who was not a Jew. What were the other taboos surrounding relationships with non-Jewish people? (Check a Bible commentary or a Bible dictionary for more help on this topic.) Ask the group:
- How did the Holy Spirit convince Peter to change his attitudes?
- What change in thinking did Peter have?
- How do we know that he really did change?
- What did we learn about Peter? (Add to Session 1 chart.)
- What did we learn about God, Jesus, and/or the Holy Spirit?

Look up these Scripture texts and talk about how they still apply to us today: Acts 10:15, 28, 34-35, 36, 47; Acts 11:17.

Provide time for the youth to think quietly about what the Holy Spirit may be telling them about accepting others who are different. Have a time of silent prayer, inviting God to help us be friends to all people. Encourage the youth to begin today to look at others through God's eyes, not their own.

3. Do an affirmation exercise that helps the youth put into practice acceptance of all people in their group. Divide into groups of two to four people. Be sure all the groups are the same size. Have on hand construction paper, magazines, clip art books (if you have a photocopier), ribbons, markers, scissors, and glue.
   a. Each group will design and make an award for each person in one of the other groups. Stress the personality gifts of the individual, not things for which they have no control, such as hair colour, height, or eye shape. Encourage the expression of positive characteristics that youth showed during the sessions together.
   b. Carry out a presentation time when the awards are given and received. Gather in a circle for presentation of the awards. Have everyone sign each person's award as a souvenir of the week together.

Take a Break
1. Serve a simple snack.
2. Play a cooperative group game. (See page 95.)

Respond
1. Take the time to complete the mobile. Review the stories of Peter's transformation from a fisherman to a bold leader in the new church. Talk about the ways that the relationship between Peter and Jesus grew. We can assume that Peter continued to change and mature as a follower of Jesus.

Have the youth think about each symbol as it relates to her or his relationship with Jesus. What would be an appropriate reminder of Jesus' wish that we value all people in the same way that God does? Some suggestions: A butterfly is a symbol of transformation, change, and freedom. Check the Make and Take Resource (pages 110-111) for several butterfly options. A dove is a sign of God's presence (flood, Jesus' baptism, Holy Spirit). It is also used to symbolize peace and harmony. Complete the mobile.

2. Invite each person to tell one thing they learned about Peter and his relationship with Jesus that will stay with them in the future.

Reflect and Remember

1. Distribute the final letter from Jesus. Allow for quiet time as the youth think about rejection and acceptance at a personal level. Suggest that they refer to the letters frequently and continue the practice of writing their thoughts and prayers to Jesus when they are at home.

2. Carry out a *Circle Session.* Sit comfortably in a circle facing each other. This activity encourages active listening, acceptance and respect for others, and expression of thoughts and feelings. Outline the "rules" for Circle Session:

    a. Each person will be allowed to speak.

    b. Each person is free to say whatever she or he wishes.

    c. No one is allowed to interrupt, argue, comment, or dispute.

    d. The leader will invite each person in turn to comment and will simply say "thank-you" when that person is finished.

    e. People are allowed to "pass" if they have no comments to give.

Ask group members to respond to these questions:

- Which activity did you like the best this week? Why?
- What is one thing you will remember about Peter?
- What did you learn about becoming friends with Jesus?
- What other comments do you wish to make?

Note: Evaluation comments about the curriculum would be appreciated by the publishers of this curriculum. Please send them to the address listed on the evaluation form, page 196.

Gather and Bless

Express your appreciation and love to the youth. Affirm them and encourage them to continue their friendship with Jesus. End with your closing blessing, the Bible memory passage, and a group hug.

Dear Friend,

This is my last "formal" letter to you. I want you to know that I will always be waiting to meet with you. Each person is special to me. You are special to me. I love you very much, even though you are not perfect. In my eyes and in God's eyes, all people are equal.

I want you to look at people through my eyes. I look on their hearts, what is inside. Can you do that too? Think and act as I do, and you will see the good in others who may seem so different from you. I believe in you and your ability to accept others. And you can count on my help. I have told you before —I have chosen you to be my friend, because I care about you and I love you.

I hope you will continue to talk to me, to write to me, and to listen to me. I can change your life if you want me to. I will always be your friend.

Your friend, Jesus

My Friends

Place a check in each box that is true for you. Write the name of the friend who qualifies in each of these categories. Write the name of someone you could befriend in the categories not checked.

I have a friend . . .

- ❏ who is 10 years older than I.
- ❏ who has blue eyes.
- ❏ who has dark skin.
- ❏ who cannot speak English well.
- ❏ who wears a hearing aid.
- ❏ who is in a wheelchair.
- ❏ who worships at a synagogue.
- ❏ who lives in a high-rise apartment.
- ❏ who does not live with two parents.
- ❏ who has AIDS.
- ❏ who does not believe in God.
- ❏ who is mentally disabled.
- ❏ whose father is in jail.
- ❏ who does not go to church.
- ❏ who was not born in North America.

CURRICULUM EVALUATION FORM

Simon Peter

Church _____

Address _____

Evaluator _____

Leadership role _____

Use of materials: Age group

_____ five-day Bible school   _____

_____ Sunday school   _____

_____ midweek classes   _____

_____ festival or retreat   _____

other_____

Describe your experience with these materials–the process, the positive aspects, the problems. (Use the back side for additional comments.)

List any suggestions to improve these materials.

Thank you. Your input is greatly appreciated.

Please return completed form to Living Stones Collection, Commission on Education, General Conference Mennonite Church, Box 347, Newton, KS 67114.